HUMAN BEHAVIOR

HUMAN BEHAVIOR

A Social Work Perspective

ROBERT BERGER

Thomas More College

RONALD FEDERICO

Iona College

and the

Westchester County
Social Work Education Consortium

Longman
New York & London

Human Behavior
A Social Work Perspective

Longman Inc., 19 West 44th Street, New York, N.Y. 10036
Associated companies, branches, and representatives
throughout the world.

Developmental Editor: Nicole Benevento
Editorial and Design Supervisor: Diane Perlmuth
Interior and Cover Design: Dan Seranno
Manufacturing and Production Supervisor: Anne Musso

Library of Congress Cataloging in Publication Data

Berger, Robert, 1937–
   Human behavior, a social work perspective.

   Bibliography: p.
   Includes index.
   1. Social case work. 2. Human behavior.
I. Federico, Ronald C. II. Title.
HV43.B45   1982   361.3′2   81-11763
ISBN 0-582-28180-6   AACR2

Manufactured in Canada
9 8 7 6 5 4 3 2 1

Acknowledgments

The authors wish to express their gratitude to the following for their assistance in helping clarify issues and develop content. They also provided valuable support and encouragement through the preparation of this manuscript.

Betty Baer and Dean Pierce of the Westchester Social Work Education Consortium.

John Cahill and Maryline Golver of Thomas More College.

Lane Akers, Nicole Benevento, Carol Camper, and Diane Perlmuth of Longman Inc.

Acknowledgment is also gratefully extended to the following sources for their permission to reprint:

Figure 2.3 reprinted with permission of Macmillan Publishing Co., Inc. From *A Modern Introduction to the Family*, revised edition. Edited by Norman W. Bell and Ezra F. Vogel. Copyright © 1968 by The Free Press.

Excerpts from pp. 68, 86–89, *Educating the Baccalaureate Social Worker*, by Betty L. Baer and Ronald Federico. Reprinted with permission from EDUCATING THE BACCALAUREATE SOCIAL WORKER, copyright © 1978, Ballinger Publishing Company.

Figure 3.1 taken from Effie Hanchett, *Community Health Assessment: A Conceptual Tool Kit* (New York: John Wiley, 1979.)

Contents

Introduction

This book is intended to help social workers and other social welfare professionals become better able to utilize knowledge as a guide to practice. Understanding human behavior in its social context in order to make informed decisions about appropriate intervention requires familiarity with an extensive and diversified body of knowledge. In carrying out this goal, several assumptions are made:

1. Knowledge is fundamental for professionally responsible helping efforts.

2. Some knowledge is more useful for practice than other knowledge. This reflects a particular stance toward the goals of practice. In this book the purposes and values of the profession of social work will be the primary context within which knowledge and practice are related. Since social work is such a wide-ranging and integrating profession, social work knowledge and practice will have utility for a variety of other social welfare professions.

3. In order to be useful for practice, concepts must be learned, related to each other, and applied to actual life situations. The practitioner must also know how to determine which concepts are most useful in specific practice situations.

4. Ultimately, not all human behavior is knowable. We encourage the student and the social work practitioner to maintain a

sense of awe and wonderment when confronted with complexities of human behavior. At the same time, this book will try to illuminate as much of this behavior and the richness of its social context as our present knowledge makes possible.

The book's three principal objectives derive from the above assumptions. These objectives are the following:

1. To systematically review and summarize concepts that have particular relevance for practice. Useful concepts have been developed by various disciplines in the biological, social, and behavioral sciences. In this book concepts will be drawn primarily from sociology, psychology, political science, economics, anthropology, and (human) biology. In addition to summarizing selected concepts, the book will discuss their utility for social work practice.

2. To develop a framework that can be used to integrate the concepts. While individual disciplines concentrate on the teaching of discrete concepts and theories, this book will focus on finding relationships between them. This will make it easier to perceive and understand human behavior as a totality rather than as discrete, or separate, actions.

3. To demonstrate how integrated knowledge may be used by social workers to establish a context for the analysis and decision making that are essential components of social work practice.

It may sound as if this book is going to be more encyclopedic than it will be. The focus is as wide-ranging as it needs to be to provide a basis for understanding human behavior useful for generalist social work practice. However, there is much that is not appropriate in such an approach. For example, though knowledge of theories of personality development is important, knowledge of abnormal psychology is much less so. This is because the generalist social worker focuses on strengthening people's resources in their social/cultural/biological richness, rather than emphasizing personality weaknesses isolated from their environment. Similarly, an understanding of organizational structures is basic to successful functioning within them, but exhaustive knowledge of organizational and administrative theories is well beyond the usual practice responsibilities of the generalist social worker.

Understanding this book, then, depends on an understanding of its view of generalist social work practice. The knowledge presented here has been selected because of its relevance to that type of practice. The view of generalist social work out of which the content of this book grows is the one developed by the Undergraduate Social Work Curriculum Development Project.* Two parts of the Project's findings are particularly significant for understanding this book: the statement of the purposes of social work and the competency areas that, taken together, define the competent generalist social worker. Each will be described below.

The Project defines the purposes of social work as follows:

> Social work is concerned and involved with the interactions between people and the institutions of society that affect the ability of people to accomplish life tasks, realize aspirations and values, and alleviate distress. These interactions between people and social institutions occur within the context of the larger societal good. Therefore, three major purposes of social work may be identified:
> 1. to enhance the problem-solving, coping, and developmental capacities of people;
> 2. to promote the effective and humane operation of the systems that provide them with resources, services, and opportunities;
> 3. to link people with systems that provide them with resources, services, and opportunities.[†]

This view of social work focuses the profession's primary responsibility on the point at which people and the institutions of society come together. People are basic to the mission of social work since the profession attempts to help them better meet their needs

---

*This project was funded by the United States Department of Health, Education, and Welfare from 1975 to 1978 for the purpose of improving the quality of undergraduate social work education. Betty L. Baer was the project director. See the project report, Betty L. Baer and Ronald C. Federico, *Educating the Baccalaureate Social Worker*, vol. I (Cambridge, Mass: Ballinger Publishing Co., 1978).

†Baer and Federico, p. 68.

and achieve their life goals. However, the profession also recognizes that people develop in, and resources and opportunities are provided or denied them through social institutions like the family, the economy, and the polity. Efforts to help people require an understanding and respect of their own goals for themselves. Helping also necessitates an understanding of how the social and physical environments operate and how these environments may need to be modified in order to support people's efforts on their own behalf. Social work helping, then, most frequently involves work at both the individual and environmental levels.

The Project's view of the purposes of social work also begins to define the breadth of knowledge used by social workers. An understanding of people is basic to social work — but an understanding of people within the social and cultural contexts in which they live. These contexts help determine *what goals* are desirable and *what strategies* can be used to attain the goals. They also help social workers understand *what resources* are available to various groups in different situations — as well as what resources are not available. Finally, they help explain *the way resources are made available* to people, an important determinant of whether or not they will be used.

People, then, are linked to idea systems and resource structures that influence their lives in important ways. However, internal biological and psychological factors are also important determinants of behavior. People's problem-solving, coping, and developmental capacities are in part established by a complex interplay between heredity and environment. The personality characteristics which develop as a result of this interaction become further variables influencing behavior. Therefore, the practice of social work as defined above is built on an understanding and use of biological, psychological, cultural, and social-structural factors.

The second part of the Undergraduate Social Work Curriculum Development Project report basic to this book is the list of competencies that every social work practitioner must have. Taken together, these competencies define what social workers must be able to do in order to carry out the purposes of the profession. Naturally, many social workers will have competencies in addition to those listed here, but every social worker should be able to do at least the following:

1. Identify and assess situations where relationships between people and social institutions need to be initiated, enhanced, restored, protected, or terminated.

2. Develop and implement a plan for improving the well-being of people based on problem assessment and the exploration of obtaining goals and available options.

3. Enhance the problem-solving, coping, and developmental capacities of people.

4. Link people with systems that provide them with resources, services, and opportunities.

5. Intervene effectively on behalf of populations most vulnerable and discriminated against.

6. Promote the effective and humane operation of the systems that provide people with services, resources, and opportunities.

7. Actively participate with others in creating new, modified, or improved service, resource, and opportunity systems that are more equitable, just, and responsive to consumers of services, and work with others to eliminate those systems that are unjust.

8. Evaluate the extent to which the objectives of the intervention plan were achieved.

9. Continually evaluate one's own professional growth and development through assessment of practice behaviors and skills.

10. Contribute to the improvement of service delivery by adding to the knowledge base of the profession as appropriate and by supporting and upholding the standards and ethics of the profession.*

---

*Baer and Federico, pp. 86–89.

These competencies enable the social work practitioner to achieve the purposes of the profession as discussed above. They reflect the profession's dual focus on people and the environments that either facilitate or obstruct their efforts to plan and attain satisfying lives. Alone, each competency includes knowledge from the social, biological, and behavioral sciences. When aggregated, they prove once again how broad is the knowledge needed by social workers. Throughout this book the purposes of social work and the competencies of the professional social worker will provide the focus for the analysis and application of knowledge. Without adequate supporting knowledge, social work practice is impoverished. Without the purposes of the profession as a guide, knowledge remains primarily theoretical, difficult to relate explicitly to practice. It is this essential link between knowledge and practice that makes the whole area of human behavior and the social environment such an important one in the social work curriculum.

Plan of this Book

This book is divided into three principal sections. The first explores in more detail the ways in which knowledge relates to practice. This includes a summary of basic concepts from the biological, behavioral, and social sciences of particular relevance to social work practice. Also presented in this section is the conceptual framework that will be used throughout the book to identify relevant concepts, relate them to each other, and derive their applicability to practice.

The second part focuses on identifying biological, social, and behavioral science concepts of particular use for generalist social work practice. These are systematically summarized and then interrelated using three integrating perspectives: systems, human diversity, and goal directed behavior.

The book's third part is concerned with the application of knowledge. The concepts discussed and integrated in Part II are used to analyze the life tasks, life resources, and potential service delivery needs of people throughout the life cycle. The book ends with a discussion of knowledge areas relevant to practice that are still only poorly developed and demand further research.

A number of resources are provided throughout the book to aid readers. Illustrations of concepts and conceptual frameworks are provided so that readers can grasp better the points being discussed in the text. Study questions are provided to guide the reader's thinking about the content of each chapter. Bibliographies for each chapter are also provided so readers can pursue in more depth topics that interest them.

Educational Outcomes

Upon completion of this book, the reader should have a better grasp of the relation between knowledge and practice. He or she should also understand the biological, psychological, cultural, and social-structural components of human behavior well enough to see practice situations automatically in those terms. But perhaps most importantly, the reader should be committed to professional helping as a thoughtful activity, one which joins caring and interpersonal skill with knowledge and professional values. Although it is systematic, practice requires more than the use of formulas. Skillful use of knowledge and analysis is needed to understand particular practice situations in all of their biological, psychological, cultural, and social-structural uniqueness.

Finally, it is hoped that this book will contribute to its readers' commitment to lifelong learning. Learning how to use knowledge for decision-making purposes can help readers become more active consumers of knowledge and more active decision makers in the course of practice activities. Understanding the complex interplay of biological, psychological, cultural, and social-structural variables, should enable readers to identify when and how systems disadvantage and demean people. Once the knowledge pertaining to particular parts of human behavior is clarified, each part can also be understood as part of a multifaceted whole.

Beyond achieving the overall objectives outlined in this chapter, it is our hope that this book will encourage and support the development of further knowledge to improve the human condition. But it is also hoped that readers will use fully the knowledge they already have at the same time that they seek to know more so that even more knowledge can be brought to the service of social work practice.

PART I

Summarizing Basic Concepts

... If you demand on the one hand, the raw material of poetry in all its rawness and that which is on the other hand genuine, you are interested in poetry.

Marianne Moore[1]

CHAPTER 1

The Conceptual Framework

Introduction

Marianne Moore's advice to the would-be poet about the importance of incorporating the "genuine" into his or her poetic vision
might well apply to the social work practitioner. An awesome task
indeed! The purview of the subject matter is so broad, the existing
body of literature in the social and behavioral sciences so tentative,
and the professional task so immediate that one can easily identify
with the dilemma of the beginning practitioner depicted by Alan
Mendelsohn:

> The realities of working with people in the vast social landscape serve
> only to identify the lack of knowledge of human beings and their en-
> vironment and force the social worker to the painful acknowledgement
> that all answers are not yet known.[2]

For a profession charged with the responsibility of addressing
pressing social problems, it would seem, in effect, to be "fiddling
while Rome burns" if we wait until all the answers are known, until
all the data is collected before charting a plan of action. We must
acknowledge the lack of absolute certitude regarding many of the
problems and issues confronting the profession and resolve to continue our quest for more and more precise knowledge. However, in
the meanwhile the practitioner must use existing knowledge to the
fullest in order to design action plans based on rational decision
making.

This chapter begins by exploring in more detail the breadth of
knowledge needed to attain the purposes of the profession discussed in the last chapter. It then presents the framework which will
be used throughout the rest of the book. This framework is one which
helps social workers identify the major specific concepts needed to
adequately understand the practice situations they face daily. It also
helps practitioners to interrelate these concepts so that human life is
seen as a complex but reasonably comprehensible whole. Finally, it
is a framework which is readily applicable to concrete life events.
After the framework is presented in this chapter, it is used and further elaborated in the remaining chapters.

Tasks of the Social Worker Relating to
Human Behavior and the Social Environment

Knowledge available to the practitioner includes both explanatory and intervention knowledge. Explanatory knowledge guides the practitioner in answering the question "why?" It has primary utility in the assessment phase of the interventive process when the social worker is trying to understand the dimensions and significant elements of a situation. Principles and concepts from anthropology, biology, economics, political science, and sociology are heavily called upon in addressing "why" questions. Intervention knowledge, useful in addressing "how" and "what" questions, calls for an integration of knowledge and practice experience. It helps practitioners decide what to do once a situation has been assessed. Joel Fischer, in discussing the importance of mastering content in both the causal-diagnostic (explanatory) and interventive areas, states:

> By definition, a professional practice rests on a body of knowledge the purpose of which is to supply the practitioner with the capacity to influence (or control or change) "natural" events. In fact, practice theory, per se, can be described as being composed of two major elements.
> The first involves a systematic explication of diagnostic principles (with the goal of understanding the phenomena of concern). The second part involves a systematic explication of principles of change, and procedures for implementing those principles. Hypothetically, the diagnostic and treatment principles are to be utilized together.[3]

Explanatory and interventive knowledge are not mutually exclusive categories, and their separation is only for clarity of presentation. In reality, issues arising in practice often are the soil from which questions for additional research grow. The relationship between knowledge and practice is a reciprocal one in that application of knowledge serves as a tool in assessing its utility. Knowledge, then, directs and informs interventive efforts, helps assess why such efforts were helpful or not, and in turn identifies gaps and weaknesses in our existing knowledge base.

Knowledge shapes and focuses the social worker's understanding of human behavior in the social environment in three interrelated and cumulative ways:

1. Familiarity with biological, social, and behavioral science concepts helps to explain the multifaceted dimensions of individual, group, and social-structural behavior. These basic concepts come from human biology, anthropology, economics, political science, psychology, and sociology.

2. Integration of concepts from the above multiple sources and identification of those with particular utility for practice help develop a holistic view of human behavior.

3. Application of integrated knowledge to concrete situations as part of one's practice guides intervention efforts.

The first of these essentially refers to "knowledge about" and as such has value to the social worker primarily when successfully incorporated with the second (integration) and third (application). Two examples will illustrate what we mean by the cumulative and interrelated nature of these uses of knowledge.

Knowledge about metabolic changes accompanying mid-life may be explored in the biological science component of the curriculum. Such changes may include changes in hormonal secretions, changes in the various organ systems, or degenerative changes that increase one's vulnerability to illness and organ dysfunction. Significance is added when the psychosocial aspects of mid-life are examined. The doubts and conflicts often associated with these physical changes take form in highly personal ways and therefore require an understanding of the life experiences of each individual. Do all men in the 40–50 year age range confront the possibility of death from coronary occlusion with a similar defensive structure? Do all women assign the same meaning to the loss of generative functions accompanying mid-life? Do sociocultural forces color the emotional impact of the "change of life" differently for men and women?

Biological and psychosocial concepts are in turn enriched through an analysis of social-structural variables that have an impact on human behavior. Comprehending the differential access to resource structures that inhibit or strengthen the individual's ability to cope with change adds an important dimension to one's understanding of what at first appears to be primarily a biological/psychological phenomenon. Socially structured racist and sexist policies, for example, influence resource systems designed to support the mutual adjustment of both the individual and society. Economic policies that keep women out of the labor force, or that restrict the jobs available to them exemplify this. Such policies may help men maintain a sense of mid-life well-being while making women's mid-life adjustments to reduced nurturing roles more difficult by limiting access to stimulating and satisfying employment.

Erikson's developmental stage of infancy with the corresponding psychosocial crisis of trust vs. mistrust serves as another example of the necessity of incorporating biological, sociocultural, and psychological content for a more complete understanding of life cycle material. George Herbert Mead's concept of significant others enhances one's understanding of the importance of primary relationships at this developmental stage. The biological research of Bowlby and the psychoanalytic studies of Anna Freud also emphasize the importance of a consistent nurturing object for the infant's sense of well-being. As in the example of mid-life adjustments, social-structural issues need to be assessed to plan effective intervention in cases involving infants. Are resources equally distributed among the population to support this developmental stage? For example, are life-sustaining and life-enriching resources equally available to all infants regardless or race or ethnicity, or whether raised by a single parent? To answer these questions it will be necessary to take into account the reciprocal relationships between biological and psychological well-being and such cultural and social-structural variables as values, the family, health care, housing, and employment.

Both examples illustrate the importance of the social worker's familiarity with concepts from a variety of sources, as well as the ability to use these concepts together to understand the totality of a situation and decide what action to take. Shifting the attention from the individual to larger social contexts makes clearer the social policy implications that need to be addressed. In this way knowledge from the biological, behavioral, and social sciences becomes, through integration and selection, practice- and policy-directed.

To use knowledge in his or her practice, the practitioner must also develop skill in assessing empirical data that support underlying concepts. Skill in research methodology including problem formulation, data collection, and data analysis supports the successfull accomplishment of this task. Simply understanding concepts from the social, biological, and behavioral sciences requires research skills. In addition, throughout one's professional life these concepts must be related to the data which either support or question their continued use. As noted earlier, practice tests knowledge so that it can be developed and used with ever greater precision. However, for this to occur, data from practice must be used to assess the knowledge which was selected in particular practice situations.

Four Sources of Human Behavior

Human behavior is enormously diverse and complex because it has four principal sources: biological, psychological, social-structural, and cultural. Thus part of human behavior is *biologically* motivated, deriving from the genetic inheritance that establishes potentials and limits for a person's behavior. For example, an infant will automatically grasp, suck, and move its limbs because of species reflexes (genetically programmed predispositions). However, an infant who is genetically brain damaged may not have certain of these reflexes — sucking, for example. In some cases such deficits can be eradicated through learning, while in others the potential for remedy is quite limited. These potentials are biologically created, although in humans certain social conditions are usually needed for them to be realized. While a genetically brain damaged child may be *unable* to move its limbs because of an organic deficit, a child who is *not* brain damaged may move its limbs only rarely because it lacks stimulation from others. Although the behavioral result may be similar in both cases, the cause is biological in one and social in the other. As will be discussed later in the book, the interaction of biological and social-structural forces is very significant. For example, brain damage may result from genetic programming as noted above. However, it may also be the result of prenatal influences (such as drugs or improper nutrition) or of birth traumas (premature birth, events occuring during delivery, and so forth).

A second source of behavior is *psychological*, resulting from a person's perceptual, cognitive, and emotional development. Humans are unique in that the amount of their behavior controlled by reflexes is limited. Most (but not all) of what we can do we have learned through the use of biological/psychological potential. Human behavior is operationalized through the development of perceptual, cognitive, and motor capacities, as well as through the development of personality structures* that mediate between individual needs and the social-structural environment. The development of psychological components is heavily dependent on human interaction — the way in which individuals relate to each other in supportive, competitive, or even destructive ways. Once psychological capacities are developed (or not developed), they become important determinants of people's patterns of behavior both individually and collectively.

Social structures represent a third source of behavior. Social structures, such as the family and the economic system, exist to organize and pattern social interaction. This structuring is essential for social order, making it possible for people to behave with some degree of predictability. Once structures exist they control behavior and exert pressures to maintain themselves, thereby creating social demands that then have to be balanced with the individual needs they are meant to serve. Indeed, the issue of balancing individual and societal needs is ever-present in human life and is inevitable given the fact that humans depend primarily on social interaction rather than on genetically programmed behavior. Thus, social structures serve to motivate behavior as well as to organize and control it.

Finally, all human behavior occurs within a *cultural* context. Culture embodies the values, knowledge, and material technology that

---

*Personality structure refers to the relatively stable behavior patterns that an individual develops, and that characterize that individual's typical response to situations. For example, some people are generally flexible and inquisitive while others are more rigid and guarded.

people learn to see as appropriate and desirable. Therefore, culture establishes the parameters that guide and often limit people's thinking and behavior. Culture becomes an even more significant influence on behavior in a society comprised of many cultural groups. United States society, for example, is composed of a diverse range of ethnic, socioeconomic, and lifestyle groups, each of which influences the thinking and behavior of its members. To the degree that the one person may belong to several cultural groups — such as a Catholic, single parent, Italian-American woman with few economic resources — cultural influences on behavior can be subtle and diverse. These influences become even more complex given the need to create a viable culture that integrates many separate groups. At several levels, then, culture is an important source of behavior.

While the four sources of human behavior discussed above can be analyzed separately for conceptual clarity, in reality they work together to shape human life. Each of us has a unique biological endowment that creates our behavior potentials. However, the degree to which our potential is realized is heavily influenced by our culture, our psychological development, and our social-structural environment. For example, a woman who is born with a high intelligence but lives in a culture that does not value intellectual achievement in women is unlikely to have many opportunities to develop her intelligence as fully as would be biologically possible. The woman's family and social class standing are important interweaving social-structural variables. If the family values the woman's intellectual achievement and has economic resources, it may be able to take advantage of whatever educational resources are available in the culture and society. On the other hand, if the family's values concur with the culture's devaluation of education for women, or if the family lacks economic resources, the woman will most likely have few opportunities to develop her intellectual potential.* Indeed, she may come to think of herself as either unintelligent or deviant if

---

*It is important to remember that the family operates within a larger societal context. If the society devalues women, the family may either reinforce such a societal value or try to shield its female members from the behavioral effects of such a value. Changing the value itself would have to occur at the societal level.

others treat her as such. Thus it is the *interaction* of biological, psychological, social-structural, and cultural sources of behavior that, generally, has most significance for an individual's life experience. Any one of them is far less important than the way each impacts on the others.

Understanding the Four Sources
of Behavior: Basic Concepts

It is possible to understand each of the four sources of behavior only after one understands the basic concepts that describe and explain specific components of behavior. These concepts are generated and codified in the major social, biological, and behavioral science disciplines, most importantly human biology, psychology, sociology, anthropology, political science, and economics. Many readers will have already studied some or all of these disciplines and have been exposed to their most important concepts. Others will be in the process of doing so. It is important to study concepts in the context of their respective disciplines. This provides the historical and methodological perspectives needed to fully understand them in all their richness.

Throughout this book concepts will be used in various combinations dictated by the need to understand helping situations in a holistic way. Again, a social worker needs to understand as many aspects of a situation as possible. As noted above, this includes the biological, psychological, social-structural, and cultural components of behavior as they interact with each other. Before concepts explaining or describing various aspects of situations can be used in the combinations necessary to understand a particular practice situation, each must be understood individually. Therefore, this section will briefly summarize some of these concepts to provide a common understanding of them. The next section will present the framework to be used in the rest of the book for the purpose of combining or integrating concepts. It is this integration of concepts that makes a holistic approach possible in practice. While this summary will provide a useful common base for the rest of the book, three cautions should be observed. This is only a *summary*. There is no substitute for the level of understanding gained from a study of these concepts in their respective disciplines. The second caution regards the *selective* nature of this summary. The concepts presented here are only a selection of those that are potentially useful in social work practice. The reader should be constantly alert to others which may also be useful. The third caution is to resist *fragmentation* of concepts, to remember that human life is a complex whole, and concepts discussed in one area (such as the biological source of behavior) frequently have applicability in other areas as well.

In order to avoid a random listing, concepts will be organized under the by now familiar headings of biological, psychological, social-structural, and cultural.* Like any organizing framework, this one is somewhat arbitrary; it has been selected in order to avoid the separateness that can be generated by disciplinary boundaries. It also reduces the framework to four parts — a manageable number. Finally, it relates directly to the framework that will be used later in this book. Before beginning, remember that this is only a *selection* of very briefly *summarized* concepts. There is no substitute for a careful study of these and other relevant concepts in the context of their respective disciplines.

Basic Biological Concepts. The most fundamental concept of human behavior is *life* itself. The physiological process of life is the management of complex chemical processes mediated by the *brain* through an elaborate series of neurological impulses. The brain serves as a command center that activates (or fails to activate) the chemical substances and their interactions that begin at *conception*. At conception a female egg is fertilized by male sperm. This union combines genetic information from the two parents in the form of

---

*Readers should consult the bibliography at the end of the chapter for titles of works providing further elaboration of the concepts used here. No attempt is made to specifically cite each one in the text itself. Such an effort would be unnecessarily tedious and repetitive.

46 *chromosomes** which then chart the newly conceived individual's *biological potential*. Each combination of genetic information is multi-generational as well as unique. It is multi-generational in that the parents carry genetic information from their parents, which may in turn be passed on to the newly conceived generation. This is true even for genetic information that is not physiologically evident in the parent as, for example, when red-haired children are born to parents neither of whom have red hair. Genetic combinations are unique in that a mixing process occurs during fertilization so that only some genetic elements of each parent become part of the newly created fetus. In addition, *mutations* may occur in genes to change them from their original form when they are transmitted at conception. While mutations are relatively rare, they and the natural genetic mixing process which occurs at conception ensure *human difference*. Thus each person is unique biologically, and this becomes an important basis for his/her social uniqueness since social development depends upon the potentials created by genetic inheritance.

Because of this genetically defined potential for behavior, human beings have tremendous *adaptation* potential. Rather than being guided primarily by genetically programmed *reflexes* that predispose the organism to react in set ways to particular situations, the human being can make use of many types of resources in many different ways. For example, nutritional needs are met by utilizing a vast variety of plant and animal substances. This flexibility makes it possible for humans to adapt to any number of geographical and climatic environments. This example demonstrates that genetic flexibility in humans is extremely far-reaching. Not only can humans physiologically process many types of nutrients (flesh, plants, and so on), they also have the capacity to *learn* how to process potential nutrients so that they can be better digested (through curing processes, cooking, and storage strategies to avoid spoilage, to name a

---

*Chromosomes are the carriers of genetic information. They are strands in the nuclei of somatic and sex cells along which genes are arranged in linear order. Genes comprise the basic unit of heredity. See Benjamin Wolman, ed., *Dictionary of Behaviorial Science* (New York: Van Nostrand Reinhold Co., 1973), pp. 61 and 156.

few). It is the complex interplay of chemical digestive processes, brain development and functioning capacity, and skeletal-muscular potential that make humans so adaptable. All of these factors are part of the genetic potential that humans as a species inherit, although each individual's particular set of potentials (and limits) is unique. As will be discussed later, part of the human inheritance is the potential for language which makes culture possible. The interaction of culture and biology then becomes extremely important in human behavior by preserving and transmitting those types of adaptations which have proven most effective.

Once created, life must be actively sustained or it will quickly end. Part of the human's genetic inheritance is a set of instructions that cause physiological *growth and development* to occur in an orderly process throughout the *life cycle*, the period of life from conception to *death* (the end of life). When the genetic plan is able to unfold because the resources needed to permit growth and development have been provided, we can talk about physiological *health*. As noted earlier, the genetic plan can accommodate extensive variation and adaptation while moving the human organism through the stages of increasing size, complexity, and autonomy that characterize growth and development. In a state of health, there is a relatively stable interaction and exchange between the various components of the human body. For example, enough blood is pumped by the heart and adequately oxygenated by the lungs to feed the muscles so that they contract and relax in the process of use that leads to their increase in size and strength. This view of the human body is a *systemic* one, focusing on the way the parts (organs, bones, muscles, blood, nerves and so on) of a whole (the biological body) work together to allow the whole to maintain itself in its environment. This relatively steady state of a system is called *homeostasis*. Obviously the concept of systems is a complex one, referring to a hierarchy of wholes of which the body is only one (others would include the family, the community, society, and so on). At a later point in the book systems will be analyzed in more detail.

Since the end of life is part of the life cycle, *degenerative processes* are part of the developmental process. As the human body ages the genetic plan begins to enact the deterioration of cells at a rate and in a pattern unique to each person. Degenerative processes are strongly affected by *stress* which pushes a person toward or beyond his or her adaptive capacity. Stress may occur at any point in the life cycle, and is often experienced in the form of inadequate *nutrition* (the basic nutrients needed for physiological health), inadequate *nurturance* (the basic protection and caring needed for psychological well-being, which strongly affects physiological health), and an environment which lacks basic life-sustaining and life-enriching resources. Stress often generates *pain* as a warning that some part of the system is being pushed toward its adaptive limit. There may also be a relationship between degenerative processes and *deficits*. The potential for growth and development may be limited, sometimes severely, by parts of the human system that are deficient or whose functioning is severely constrained. This can be due to genetic inheritance or traumas of living, such as accidents. Brain damage, for example, is a deficit that affects the whole neurological structure and the ability of the brain to manage other physiological processes. The existence of major physical deficits often interacts with and accelerates the degenerative processes that are a natural part of the life cycle.

Life ends in *death*, the point at which the human body is no longer able to sustain itself. Death is inevitable and is the result of genetically programmed patterns. Death may also be caused by stress that pushes the body beyond its adaptive limits — the *trauma*, or shock, of blood loss caused by an accident, for example. Although conception and death are fundamentally biological processes, their significance is most often defined by the social context in which they occur. For example, the deaths of an infant, a middle-aged breadwinner, and an elderly person have very different impacts on other individuals and social groups, such as family members and family units. In moving now to basic psychological concepts (and then social-structural and cultural ones), it is important to recall that human behavior is only understandable as the interplay of biological, psychological, social-structural, and cultural factors.

Basic Psychological Concepts. People's responses to their environment are dependent on their understanding of it, which is the result of psychological processes combining biological and social factors. In terms of understanding the environment, three biologically-based capacities are of particular importance. *Perception* is the ability to see, hear, smell, feel, and touch. These make it possible for people to respond to the sensory characteristics of their environment in ways that permit organized responses to them. *Cognition* is the ability to process and organize sensory information in order to manipulate the environment to achieve one's own goals. *Emotion*, or *affect*, are the feelings that become attached to information derived from perceptions and cognitive functioning. All three — perception, cognition, and affect – have physiological roots. The workings of the eye, the functioning of the brain, and hormonal responses to a threatening situation are all examples. However, the social environment is obviously a powerful factor in the ways these biologically-based capacities develop and are used, demonstrating again the close interaction of biological and social sources of behavior.

The flexibility with which humans are blessed due to their genetic inheritance adds another dimension to perception, cognition, and affect. The social environment in which people live attributes particular meaning to certain events and objects. These meanings are learned through the process of *socialization*, the way we learn what we are expected to do and how we are to accomplish it. While we can see and hear with great acuity given our rather sophisticated physiological equipment, we gradually learn to pay particular attention to those parts of the environment that are most significant for us. As infants, for instance, we learn to distinguish the primary care given from others around us. Similarly, we use our cognitive capacities to learn to do some things and are relatively unconcerned about learning to do others. While Europeans commonly learn several languages because of their close geographical proximity to other countries, the relative geographical isolation of the United States has tended to make this less of a perceived concern. Thus the perceptions and areas of cognitive development identified as important influence the amount of affect, or emotional investment, accorded them. People perceived as important evoke feelings of affection or respect. Situations that we have learned are threatening or confusing become associated with feelings of apprehension, fear, or inadequacy.

Gradually the physiological potentials for perception, cognition, and emotion become part of the individual's response to the environment. *Personality* is the integrating psychological structure that develops to help the individual function in the environment. Personality is comprised of fairly consistent patterns of responses to situations. While some people see threatening situations as dangerous, others respond to them with excitement. Some people express anger very directly, while others find it difficult to let people know when they are angry. In these and countless other ways people differ in their responses to situations according to their personality characteristics. The personality's task of mediating between the individual and the environment is closely related to the individual's needs. Some needs are primarily physical, like eating and resting. Others are much more social, such as feeling secure, competent, and loved. Needs are most often *learned* through *interaction* with others. While we must eat to live, we learn what to eat, how to prepare it, how to eat it, and when to eat it. This learning occurs in interaction with others through the process of socialization discussed above. Behavior is taught through the *conditioning* that occurs in interaction. Interaction which rewards us for our behavior strengthens it, while negative responses to our behavior generally weaken it. However, people's interpretations differ on what interaction is rewarding and what is negative.

Once needs have been learned, they become powerful *motivations* for behavior. Most people try to maximize experiences they perceive as pleasurable, and having one's needs met is usually seen in this way. People are, therefore, motivated to engage in need-meeting behavior. As noted earlier, definitions of needs to be met (both physical and social) and appropriate ways of meeting them are learned through interaction and conditioning. Personality develops as a person learns how to use his or her genetically created perceptual and cognitive abilities to meet needs in order to experience pleasurable physical sensations and social approval. In managing the interaction of the person and the environment so that need-meeting can occur, various *defenses* are used. These include projection, repression, sublimation, reaction formation, regression, and others. Defenses help the personality keep a balance between the desires of the individual and the demands of the environment. De-

fenses are functional tools for the personality except when they become so rigid and elaborate that they block the individual's ability to
perceive accurately physical needs or social reality.

It should be increasingly evident that the boundaries between
biological, psychological, social-structural, and cultural sources of
human behavior are very fluid. The biological foundations of behavior are basic to life, but the ways environmental conditions affect
those foundations are powerful determinants of the developing personality. The personality, in turn, becomes a very significant factor
in perceiving and meeting biological needs through the use of environmental resources. The personality also interprets social needs
and guides a person's efforts to respond to them. As a system of
interacting biological, psychological, social-structural, and cultural
components, the human being is very complex. The larger systems
created by the interaction of great numbers of people become even
more so. We will now turn to the concepts which focus on these
larger systems.

Basic Social-Structural Concepts. *Social structure,* or *social organization,* refers to the ways in which social behavior becomes patterned and predictable. Underlying the concept of social structure is
the belief that social behavior is, for the most part, organized and
non-random. Several kinds of patterning occur. *Social institutions*
are especially important parts of the social structure, organizing
activities around particular *social purposes* or *functions.* For example, as a social institution, the family organizes categories of people
— such as mothers, fathers, husbands, wives, sons, daughters,
cousins, mothers-in-law, and so forth — around the performance of
functions essential to the survival of society: reproduction, socialization and care of the young, education, primary group relationships,
and of decision making about economic resources. Other social institutions include education, religion, politics, economics, and social
welfare — each of which organizes the behavior of large numbers of
people around social functions. *Roles* refer to the expected behavior
of categories of people within social institutions, so we can look at
the role of mothers, the role of sons, and so on. Most people participate in many social institutions and occupy many roles at the same

time. Sometimes the demands of these multiple roles conflict and cause difficulty for people who are attempting to perform them.

The functions, or purposes, of social institutions are often partly *manifest* (publicly stated and assumed to be for the good of society as a whole) and partly *latent* (less public and more beneficial for some groups in society than for others). For example, the manifest function of social welfare as a social institution is to provide basic resources for those lack them. However, the point is often made that the latent function is to control people (especially minority groups and the poor) by manipulating the resources provided and the ways they are made available. In part this relates to the nature of relationships between people and groups in a social structure. *Cooperative* interaction maximizes the focus on the good of society as a whole, whereas *competitive* interaction encourages people to focus on their own good. *Conflict* can carry competition into the realm of actively destructive behavior by one group in relation to others.

Social structures rarely treat everyone equally. Usually there is some type of *social differentiation* in which criteria are used to distinguish between groups of people. Commonly used criteria are age, sex, race, ethnicity, and physical characteristics such as size, "looks," and the presence or absence of deficits, or handicaps. While such differentiation can be used simply to relate ability to activity — children are not allowed to drive because they lack the ability to do so, for example — it may also be used to stratify people. *Social stratification* refers to the process of ranking people in terms of socially defined criteria. A stratification process is a type of *hierarchy*, a vertical arrangement of people on the basis of access to resources. Those with access to resources usually have power. *Power* is the ability of a person or group to enforce its will on others, and it may be based in *authority* (legitimate power) or illegitimate *coercion*, or *force*. The importance of power is the control it confers over *resources* which are socially defined as valuable. There is, then, a reciprocal relationship between power and access to resources. Resources can include practically anything — money, diamonds, gold, food, reputation, goat skins, old furniture, physical size or appearance, land, weapons, and on and on. Those in power control the *decision making* which establishes the *policies* determining the production and distribution of many resources.

Access to basic life-sustaining resources is essential for survival. Such resources are made available through the *economic* institution, which has as its major social functions extracting natural resources from the environment, producing goods from them, distributing those goods, and providing needed services. These functions are performed through the use of land, labor, capital, entrepreneurship, and technology. Those with power have more control over and access to economic processes. Therefore, they have more goods and services as well as decision-making power to protect their privileged position. In our own society, access to *money* is the single most important factor in ensuring access to basic life-sustaining resources. The *poor* have little money and thus limited ability to get the resources they need. That is why poor people experience higher rates of disease, death, crime, social isolation, unemployment, and low levels of schooling. *Poverty*, then, is the chronic lack of life-sustaining and life-enriching resources. *Social class* is the stratification process that ranks people according to their access to such life-sustaining and life-enriching resources.

To understand poverty and social class, two factors are especially important. One is the nature of economic processes themselves. When problems occur in the relationships between the use of land, labor, capital, entrepreneurship, and technology, large scale economic problems are likely to result. This is what happens during recessions and depressions, affecting people at all social class levels (although the poor are generally affected first and most severely). The second factor is social differentiation. When social differentiation is tied to social stratification, a situation is created in which power is used by some groups (called the *dominant or majority groups*) to maintain their own privilege (access to resources) at the expense of other groups (called *minority groups*). In our own society men, those of Western European backgrounds, Caucasians, the rich, and heterosexuals are dominant, while women, other racial and ethnic groups,* the poor, the elderly, those with physical de-

---

*A race is a large population group that shares *hereditary characteristics* passed down from generation to generation. An ethnic group is a population group which shares a *culture*, although it may also have some common hereditary characteristics.

ficits, and homosexuals are minorities. Membership in a minority group increases the likelihood that one's access to resources will be limited. For example, women and Black people are discriminated against when seeking high-paying and prestigious jobs (or, for that matter, graduate education to prepare for such jobs). We can see, then, that there is a clear relationship between social differentiation, social stratification, power, and access to socially desirable resources.

One last correlate of power and social differentiation is important for social workers to understand — *social control*. Social control are the procedures used by a social structure to maintain order, since disorder threatens the structure itself. Naturally those persons who occupy positions of power are concerned with preserving the existing social structure since they benefit most from it. Those who have limited access to social resources and who feel they cannot increase their access may believe they have little to lose by challenging the existing social structure. Hence, social control mechanisms are often seen as repressive by minority group members. Social control mechanisms include *socialization* (teaching people only socially acceptable ways to behave), *social sanctions* (socially defined positive or negative responses to behavior), and physical force such as is vested in the criminal justice structure.

Finally, something which has been implicit in the preceding parts of this section must now be explicitly addressed. As is probably obvious, social structures organize individual behavior through *groups*. A group is two or more people who have a sense of common purpose and interact on a regular basis. There are many kinds of groups and many specific aspects of group structure that affect the behavior of group members (decision making, leadership, group purpose, and so forth). Of particular significance is whether a group is *primary* or *secondary*. A primary group is generally small and is characterized by intensive, face-to-face interaction. Primary groups may be goal directed at times, but they are also forums in which their members seek to have their basic needs met for acceptance and care. Secondary groups are larger and generally more impersonal, focused more on goal attainment than on meeting members' basic needs. Especially important secondary groups are *formal organizations* or *bureaucracies*. These group structures have clearly identified goals and means to attain them, a hierarchical structure of relationships, an emphasis on jobs, or positions, rather than the specific people who perform the jobs at any particular time, and the expectation that interaction between members will be around performing the job rather than personal wishes or needs.

Formal organizations dominate a society like our own. Indeed, most social work and social welfare services are provided through such structures. Therefore, it is important for social workers and anyone seeking help to learn how to function effectively in formal organizations. The demands can be severe, making access to primary groups an important antidote to the strains of large scale secondary groups like formal organizations. Once again we see the critical task for social work of focusing on the point at which the individual and the environment come together. The social structure determines how resources will be made available, and to whom. Groups mediate between the individual and the social structure as a whole. Linking back to earlier sections, we can see how biology generates potential that is developed through psychological means and enriched or restricted in the environment managed by the social structure.

Basic Cultural Concepts.   When we think most broadly about our environment, we usually think of society. However, *culture* is even broader than society. Culture is the storehouse of values, knowledge, and material objects that a group has accumulated and preserved over generations. Society is a geographical area in which a culture is used and made operational through a social structure. Using our own society as an example, we can clearly identify the geographical boundaries of the United States. We can also describe the values, ways of doing things, and technology characteristic of our society as a whole. For example, we do not sacrifice virgins to deities, we speak our own version of English — somewhat different from the English spoken in Great Britain — we drive on the right side of the road, we generally find nuclear energy acceptable, and most of us like air conditioning when it is hot. All these parts of our culture are translated into specific behaviors, rules for behavior, and organizational procedures that characterize our day-to-day behavior in this society.

It has no doubt occurred to you that there are variations among groups in the way people think and act. This is due to *subcultures*, smaller groups existing within the larger group that have some unique cultural characteristics. Italian Americans, for example, have different values and behaviors with respect to the family than do Native Americans. However, these differences can coexist within the larger culture in such a way as to preserve the overarching characteristics of the larger culture. This harmonious coexistence of different subcultural groups is called *cultural pluralism*. When one subcultural (or cultural) group questions the appropriateness of the way another is structured or evaluates another group on the basis of its own cultural elements, it is called *ethnocentrism*. Social workers have to remember that the cultural integrity of each subcultural group is the only appropriate context for understanding that group's behavior. That some elements of a subculture may create difficulties for its members in the larger culture does not mean either group is right or wrong. But it requires careful negotiation to see that the needs of both groups are met in ways appropriate for each.

Ethnocentrism is sometimes the cause of definitions of *deviance*. A culture's, or subculture's, values generate *norms*, or rules for behavior. Behavior that violates these norms is considered unacceptable or deviant. Once again it is important to note that behavior can only be judged acceptable or unacceptable when it is evaluated according to some standard. When groups have different standards, created by differences in their cultures, they may have difficulty accepting each other's behavior. For example, management of time in many Hispanic and Black subcultures is different from that in our dominant culture. This sometimes leads members of the dominant group to accuse Hispanics and Blacks of being deviant by being late for appointments or unconcerned about "efficiency." Obviously there is nothing inherently right or wrong about any group's management of time. It is only right or wrong with respect to some standard, and different cultural/subcultural groups often have different standards, or norms. Clearly power becomes a relevant factor in these situations, since the dominant group may attempt to impose its standard on others.

Power conflicts are often couched in terms of right and wrong, which is simply another way of saying normative and deviant. While a group with power may be able to *label* another group deviant, and persecute or otherwise control it as a result, the social worker must be able to separate ethnocentrism from cultural pluralism. Whether or not the social worker is successful in helping a minority group avoid being labeled and treated as deviant, he or she should at least be clear that there is nothing inherently wrong with a particular group's behavior. When discussing biological concepts, it was noted that difference is built into humans through the genetic process. Culture also builds in difference through the creation of alternatives in social behavior. However, a dominant group's definitions of normativeness and deviance may ignore these quite natural sources of difference. Short men may be devalued even though size is a natural biological variation. Similarly, sexually active women may be devalued even though various cultures and subcultures treat sexual behavior quite differently.

Culture is a powerful influence on behavior since it serves to organize a society's social structure, which then governs people's actions. Once again we come back to the continuum from biological through cultural behavior. Human behavior is an interlocking whole in which each source influences the others. While we may begin our analysis of behavior in any of the four sources, sooner or later we must place it in its larger context. If we fail to do so, we have not looked at the question holistically and will therefore have difficulty focusing on the purpose of social work: to help people function more effectively in their environment. Each concept discussed in this section helps us understand some particular part of human behavior. Each deserves careful study, here and in the context of its respective discipline. But how are they all to be interrelated to become useful, practical tools for attaining the purposes of social work? The next section will address the need to relate all of these concepts to each other so practice is supported by a holistic view of human behavior.

The Integrating Framework

Human behavior is a whole in which some parts are initiated and maintained biologically, others psychologically, and still others socially and culturally. Social workers need to view the practice situations they encounter in a way that incorporates these four sources of behavior. Such a view must focus on the holistic quality of human behavior at the same time that it recognizes the many different ways that the biological, psychological, social, and cultural components of that behavior can be put together by people to identify and strive toward life goals. Seen diagrammatically, the social work view of practice might look as follows:

FIGURE 1.1

Human Behavior and Social Work Practice

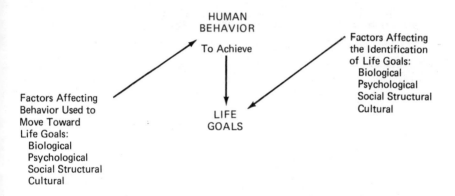

For a social worker to make informed decisions about how to intervene in a practice situation, he or she must understand the relationship between all these parts of the situation.

When we talk about biological, psychological, social-structural, and cultural factors affecting human behavior and efforts to identify and achieve life goals, we must recognize that these factors can either serve as *resources*[4] or as *obstacles*. For example, biological factors influencing behavior serve as resources when they facilitate people's ability to achieve life goals. At the species level, humans utilize a wide variety of adaptive behaviors when attempting to satisfy a need. At the individual level, high intelligence enables a person to learn quickly how to analyze and understand complex situations. On the other hand, these same factors can be obstacles when they make it more difficult for people to achieve life goals. Because humans have few genetically programmed reflexes, they are heavily dependent on each other for physical care and social learning. Those people who are isolated from others for social or biological reasons or who have few opportunities to learn from others are severely restricted in their efforts to identify and move toward life goals. Similarly, people of high intelligence may actually be at a disadvantage in situations requiring the strict observance of rules and the performance of highly routinized activities.

How can a social worker best analyze the biological, psychological, social-structural, and cultural sources of behavior to understand when and how they function as resources and obstacles? A three-part framework suggests itself as a way of easily accomplishing this task. Looking at a situation holistically enables us to examine how its various components interact in ways that create resources, obstacles, or both. We will use a *systems* perspective* to provide us with such a holistic view. Secondly, we can focus on ways that biologically and socially created differences affect the manner in which situations are perceived and experienced by different people. This helps us to understand how similar biological, psychological, social-structural, and cultural factors become resources for some and obstacles for others. We will use a *human diversity* perspective to make us alert to the sources and effects of such differences. Third, seeing human behavior as goal-directed aids us in our search for order and patterns in human behavior that sometimes seems highly idiosyncratic and even illogical. Resources and obstacles can then be analyzed in terms of human purpose as defined by the actors in social situations themselves. We will use *goal-directed behavior* as a perspective that maintains our focus on purpose. These relationships can be diagrammed in the following way:

---

*Perspective is being used in this book according to Anne Minahan's definition: "Perspectives are ways to think about and visualize situations." Her analysis of the difference between theories, perspectives, and concepts is a very helpful one, and is recommended to the reader. See Anne Minahan, "Theories and Perspectives for Social Work," *Social Work*, November 1980 (vol. 25, No. 6), p. 435.

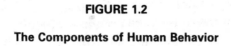

FIGURE 1.2

The Components of Human Behavior

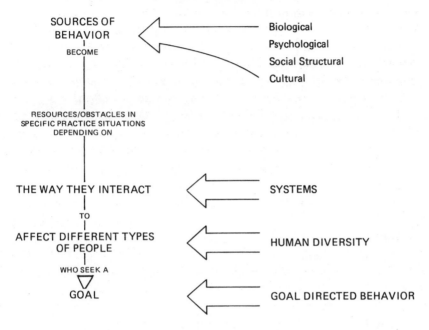

The framework to be used throughout the rest of the book, then, is built around systems, human diversity, and goal-directed behavior. When analyzing a practice situation, this framework directs the practitioner to examine the systems involved, the elements of diversity involved, and the goal being sought. In order to apply these three perspectives to a practice situation, the social worker needs to be aware of the biological, psychological, social-structural, and cultural components of each. By using the three perspectives and the sources of behavior together, the resources and obstacles existing or potentially available in a practice situation can be identified. For example, let us consider the social worker trying to help parents who have abused their children. We will use the systems perspective to see how one aspect of helping such clients to develop more effective parenting skills can be better understood. Biological characteristics of the parent or children could be a significant source of stress which might lead to abusive behavior. A hyperactive child may make demands on parents which they feel unable to meet. A parent suffering from malnutrition may lack the energy necessary to perform even minimal parenting tasks. In both cases, child abuse may be used to control the child's behavior so that it is seen as manageable by the struggling parent. In this example, biological characteristics are tied to their causes (such as inadequate nutrition) as well as their social behavior (child abuse). In this way, the systems perspective has helped to identify significant biological characteristics of a situation in order to better understand how they interact with other aspects of that situation. A more holistic view results. Existing or potential resources and obstacles are also easier to identify. If inadequate nutrition is an obstacle to effective parenting, financial, medical, and educational services are some of the resources needed to help solve the problem. To understand a practice situation such as the one above in its totality, of course, the human diversity and goal-directed behavior perspectives would also have to be applied.

The framework being proposed uses knowledge in an integrated manner to understand practice situations holistically and is diagrammed on page 29.

It is important to remember that all three perspectives are critical to a holistic view of any practice situation. The particular concepts* highlighted by each perspective in conjunction with the different sources of behavior will vary from situation to situation. For example, human diversity may emphasize the social effects of power, while goal-directed behavior may be more focused on needs as they are psychologically perceived. This, of course, is the value of the three perspectives for helping social workers integrate knowledge in order to understand human behavior holistically.

---

*The concepts referred to here are those reviewed under the four sources of behavior, such as genetics, personality, role, norm, and so on.

FIGURE 1.3

Framework for Using Knowledge to Understand Practice Situations Holistically

PERSPECTIVES FOR A HOLISTIC VIEW	SOURCES OF BEHAVIOR AND THEIR SITUATIONAL EFFECTS							
	BIOLOGICAL		PSYCHOLOGICAL		SOCIAL-STRUCTURAL		CULTURAL	
	Resource	Obstacle	Resource	Obstacle	Resource	Obstacle	Resource	Obstacle
SYSTEMS								
HUMAN DIVERSITY								
GOAL-DIRECTED BEHAVIOR								

Summary

The framework presented above will be elaborated and used throughout the rest of the book. It will be the major vehicle for attaining the book's objectives. In the perspective developed in this chapter, practice is rooted in professional purpose aimed toward improving transactions between people and environments. Knowledge geared toward developing competencies in understanding and influencing these transactions comes from several disciplines and demands of the practitioner the ability to select, integrate, and apply information from diverse sources.

At this point it is important to get a sense of the overall framework, especially in terms of how each part relates to the others. It is also important to understand how the framework relates to the purposes of the profession of social work. In the chapters that follow, specific parts of the framework will be analyzed in detail. In this way, you will soon gain a comfortable knowledge about the framework and how it is used.

Study Questions

1. About which of the four sources of behavior (biological, psychological, social-structural, and cultural) do you feel most knowledgeable? Why do you know more about these than about the others? Does this tell you something about cultural values, education as a social institution, and your own interests and experiences? How committed are you to expanding your knowledge in those areas in which you are presently less knowledgeable? How might you do so?

2. When are you most likely to consciously assess your resources? Have you ever thought of them as including biological, psychological, social-structural, and cultural components? Thinking of them in this way, do you consider that you have more or fewer resources than you had previously thought? How about obstacles — do you see more or less of these in your life using the framework presented in this chapter?

3. Thinking about obstacles, again, identify one group of people for each type of obstacle (that is, biological, social-structural, psychological, and cultural) who you feel have the most serious of that type of obstacle to overcome. Explain what these obstacles are and why you consider them especially important in terms of their effects on the lives of the people involved. Do you think others would agree with your selection of the groups with the most severe obstacles? Why or why not? Finally, can you also identify resources each group might use in coping with the obstacles you have identified?

4. Carel Germain states that the professional purpose of social work "arises from a dual, simultaneous concern for the adaptive potential of people and the nutritive qualities of their environment."[5] Calling this an ecological approach, she elaborates by pointing out that it is "concerned with the growth, development, and potentialities of human beings and with the properties of their environment that support or fail to support the expression of human potential."[6] Why do you think Germain would have chosen the concept of ecology as the best one to use when examining transactions between people and the environment? What other concepts could she have used? Having analyzed the alternatives, do you think she made a wise choice?

5. Thinking in terms of transactions suggests an exchange between the parties involved in the transaction. Why is this an important part of our thinking as social workers about the relationships people have with their environment? Can people exist without exchanging anything with the environment? Use examples of real life situations to support your answer. What are the different implications for social work if people *do* or *do not* engage in transactions/exchanges with their environment?

Notes

1.   Marianne Moore, "Poetry," in *Selected Poems* (New York: Macmillan, 1935), p. 37.

2.   Allan R. Mendelsohn, *The Work of Social Work* (New York: New View-points, 1980), p. 80.

3.   Joel Fischer, *Interpersonal Helping: Emerging Approaches for Social Work Practice* (Springfield, Ill.: Charles C. Thomas Publishers, 1973), p. XXV.

4.   Max Siporin defines a resource as follows: "any valuable thing, on reserve or at hand, that one can mobilize and put to instructional use in order to function, meet a need, or resolve a problem." Max Siporin, *Introduction to Social Work Practice* (New York: The Macmillan Co., 1975), p. 22.

5.   Carel B. Germain, ed., *Social Work Practice: People and Environments — An Ecological Approach* (New York: Columbia University Press, 1979), p. 8.

6.   Carel B. Germain and Alex Gitterman, *The Life Model of Social Work Practice* (New York: Columbia University Press, 1980), p. 5.

Additional Readings

Commoner, Barry. *The Poverty of Power: Energy and the Economic Crisis.* New York: Knopf, 1976.

Coser, L. and Rosenberg, B., eds. *Sociological Theory.* 4th ed. New York: Macmillan, 1976.

Coser, Lewis. *The Functions of Social Conflict.* New York: Free Press, 1964.

Freire, Paulo. *Pedagogy of the Oppressed.* New York: Seabury Press, 1970.

Gouldner, Alvin W. *The Coming Crisis of Western Sociology.* New York: Basic Books, 1970.

Gross, M. *The Psychological Society.* New York: Random House, 1977.

Hall, Edward. *Beyond Culture.* Garden City, N.Y.: Anchor Press, 1977.

Hall, William and Young, Christine L., eds. *Genetic Disorders: Social Service Interventions.* Pittsburgh: University of Pittsburgh Graduate School of Public Health, 1977.

Harris, M. *Cannibals and Kings: The Origin of Cultures.* New York: Random House, 1977.

Herand, Brian J. *Sociology and Social Work.* Oxford: Pergamon Press, 1970.

Hilgard, E. and Bower, G. *Theories of Leraning.* 4th ed. Englewood Cliffs, N. J.: Prentice-Hall, 1975.

Johnson, Harriette C. *Behavior, Psychopathology, and the Brain.* New York: Curriculum Concepts, 1980.

Katz, D. and Kahu, R. L. *The Social Psychology of Organizations.* 2nd ed. New York: John Wiley, 1978.

Lenski, Gerhard. *Human Societies*. New York: McGraw-Hill, 1970.
Lidz, Theodore. *The Person: His and Her Development Throughout the Life Cycle*. Rev. ed. New York: Basic Books, 1976.
Maslow, Abraham. *Toward a Psychology of Being*. 2nd ed. New York: Van Nostrand Reinhold, 1968.
Merton, Robert K. *Social Theory and Social Structure*. Rev. ed. New York: Free Press, 1957.
Mills, C. Wright. *The Sociological Imagination*. London: Oxford University Press, 1959.
Perlman, Helen Harris. *Persona: Social Role and Personality*. Chicago: University of Chicago Press, 1968.
Rose, Arnold. *The Power Structure*. New York: Oxford University Press, 1967.
Ryan, William. *Blaming the Victim*. New York: Random House, 1972.
Schiller, Bradley R. *The Economics of Poverty and Discrimination*. 2nd ed. Englewood Cliffs, N. J: Prentice-Hall, 1976.
Strelen, Herbert S. *Personality Theory and Social Work Practice*. Metuchen, N. J.: Scarecrow Press, 1975.
Sundel, Martin and Sundel, Sandra Stone. *Behavior Modification in the Human Services: A Systematic Introduction to Concepts and Applications*. New York: John Wiley and Sons, 1975.
Tussing, A. Dale. *Poverty in a Dual Economy*. New York: St. Martin's Press, 1975.
Underwood, Jane H. *Human Variation and Human Micro Evolution*. Englewood Cliffs, N. J: Prentice-Hall, 1979.
Warren, Roland L. *The Community in America*. 3rd ed. Chicago: Rand McNally, 1978.
Weinstein, Deena and Weinstein, Michael A. *Choosing Sociology: An Introduction to Critical Inquiry*. New York: David McKay, 1976.

PART II

Integrating Concepts for Practice

I am part of the sun as my eye
is part of me. That I am part of
the earth my feet know
perfectly, and my blood is part
of the sea.

D. H. Lawrence[1]

CHAPTER 2

Systems Thinking: An Integrating Tool

Introduction

The previous chapter presented an overview of selected concepts from the social, behavioral, and biological sciences that have special significance for the human services professions. The task confronting the human service practitioner attempting to assimilate the myriad concepts available from these disciplines and translate them into workable and concrete practice principles is a monumental one. Keeping abreast of current developments in socio-behavioral research in itself is a job well beyond the capacity of the average practitioner. The social work literature of the last two decades speaks increasingly of the need to develop a model in the sense of a "visual representation of how things actually work or should work under ideal conditions."[2] According to this definition, if a model is to be useful to the profession, it needs to be descriptive — accurately present the reality it attempts to explain — and prescriptive — providing a sound basis for directing change efforts toward behaviorally specific goals.

A systems approach is such a model. It is a convenient frame of reference with which to make sense of a vast amount of material from various sources and dealing with multiple levels of phenonema simultaneously. Egan and Cowan further contend a model "must be complex enough to account for the reality it attempts to describe and portray and simple enought to use,"[3] and that it must be a map for the delivery of service. A system, then, is a model used to describe reality.

Models, however, are abstractions. They do not exist "in fact" nor do they have a specific referent in the world of people, places, and events that makes up the day-to-day reality of the social worker. If the model clearly and accurately reflects the reality it attempts to describe it is potentially beneficial to the practitioner. We find the systems model useful in the sense that it fulfills the descriptive and prescriptive criteria presented above. The term *systems thinking* as used in this chapter refers to a way of employing the systems model to organize content about human behavior and the social environment with the goal of better understanding intervention. The selected ideas and concepts presented in this chapter have their origin in general systems theory, a body of theory shared by many disciplines and professions including social work.

The systems way of thinking about the world is at once *contextual* and *interactional*. By contextual we mean the social worker attempts to understand behavior in terms of the context in which it occurs. The behavior of individuals, for instance, occurs within a sociocultural context. By interactional we mean the social worker is concerned with the interactions between people and the human and non-human systems that make up their environments. Indeed the quality of this interaction is one of the central concerns of social work.

It is not the intent here to exhaust the literature on systems, nor to present systems theory in all its complexity. Instead, the intent is to discuss some ideas and concepts stemming from general systems theory that have particular value for the study of human behavior and the social environment. This chapter will present the rationale for using a systems approach, relate the use of systems thinking to professional purpose, and discuss the systems characteristics of boundary, purpose, exchange, and network as related to the biological, psychological, social-structural and cultural dimensions of behavior. Upon completion of this chapter the student will be able to more effectively deal with the vast amount of information sources available to the social worker.

Systems Theory and Professional Purpose

The struggle to bring unity out of chaos is deeply rooted in the human experience. The history of science evidences humankind's propensity to grapple with ideas, explore the relationships between them, ask questions, gather evidence, establish patterns, and grope for solutions — however tentative — that may help us better understand the world and our place in it. The physical and the social sciences share the belief that the universe has some underlying order and that behavior, be it the behavior of atomic particles or interacting individuals, is a patterned, regulated activity that can be understood and in many instances predicted and controlled. Events that, taken singly, appear random and isolated often become understand-able in the context of which they are a part.

Systems thinking offers the profession the analytical tools necessary to conceptualize the person-in-situation gestalt central to professional purpose and consistent with an ecological perspective of social work. Assessment and intervention between the individual and societal institutions challenges the profession to develop a theoretical base focusing on multiple levels of phenomena simul-taneously. Historically this has been a difficult task, as our tendency to view the world in linear and static terms has resulted in a percep-tion of professional purpose that alternates its focus between the individual and the society, rather than looking at both simultaneous-ly. Social work literature is replete with examples of how such a polarized perspective kindles the fire of the individualized-treatment-versus-social-action argument that continues, perhaps needlessly, to plague the profession. Linear approaches assume direct cause and effect relationships. In terms of causation such approaches tend to oversimplify complex issues. Intervention plans are consequently based on an oversimplified interpretation of a complex reality. Systems thinking, focusing on the interaction be-tween individual and environmental forces, helps the professional abandon these linear approaches, presenting the same phenomena in terms of the dynamic relationship between the components in interaction.

Systems: Definitions and Perspective

Systems theory is helpful to the social worker in the struggle to in-corporate information from the multiple sources already discussed into a coherent whole. A systems approach is inherently multidisci-plinary and calls the practitioner to draw from many social, be-havioral, and biological disciplines rather than having an allegiance to any one discipline. Viewing the individual in interaction with en-vironmental forces sharpens our focus for both assessment and in-tervention purposes and supports a process view of life consistent with professional purpose.

Before getting into formal definitions of systems it might be helpful to get an overview of the idea of systems. Basic to the idea of systems is the belief that units do not exist in isolation. Any unit we wish to analyze — physical, biological, or social — exists within a context which affects it, and which it, in turn, affects. Representing systems in hierarchical terms, we see small systems, such as individuals, families, and small groups, responding to and mutually influencing larger and more complex systems, such as neighborhoods, communities, and economic and political structures. A system is both a part and a whole. A neighborhood can be analyzed, for instance, as a whole or as a part of a larger whole — a city. The systems model helps us understand the reciprocal interaction between systems of varying size and complexity. Political and economic structures, for example, impact on the lives of people. People in turn directly and indirectly influence these political and economic structures. Two specific examples will further explain what we mean by systems.

The Human Body. The body is a biological system composed of highly complex and sophisticated chemicals that interact to create the organs and biological processes that make human life possible. The body, however, is dependent on obtaining certain substances from outside itself — air, water, and food, for example. In addition, bodily processes are vulnerable to other external forces, such as temperature and physical traumas (blows which break the skin or the bones, for instance). Thus we can see again that we must describe a unit (in this case the human body) in terms of its internal components (blood, bones, chemical reactions, and so forth) and its relationships with other external units (the physical world, non-human animal life, and other humans). The regulation of bodily fluids and body temperature further exemplifies the interaction between the mechanisms of the human body and external environmental forces. Fluid evaporating from the body through perspiration must be replaced, as must the salt which is also lost through perspiration. Life itself is dependent upon the quality of the interation between the physical body and external environmental forces.

The Family. The family is a social system composed of people who interact with each other in certain ways. A systems perspective views the members of a family not as isolated units but as interacting members. The ways in which they interact are determined by cultural expectations (who should raise the children, who should be the wage earner), socially structured situations (whether there is enough money to provide food for all family members), and the biological and psychological characteristics of the members themselves (such as physical handicaps or emotional needs). The family, then, like the human body, can be described internally, or in terms of its components, and externally, or in terms of its relationships with its environment. We might note at this point that the family as a unit is made up of other units — individual members, for example. These individuals can then be further subdivided into component parts, thus suggesting the complexity of levels of interactions which can result.

We can call each unit of analysis a system — in the above examples, the human body and the family are both systems. Internal components and processes within each system further define the essence of the system, as do the systems' vital relationships with other systems. Systems describe reality by describing the structure and processes *internal* to a system as well as those which *link* one system to another. These two aspects of the way systems help us describe and understand reality are especially important for understanding a phenomenon as complex as human behavior. Both examples further point out how small units, here families, are nestled within larger, more complex units, such as social institutions.

Given this overview of systems, we can now look at the concept in more detail. Definitions of systems range from von Bertalanffy's "sets of elements standing in interaction"[4] to Hall and Fagen's "set of objects together with relationships between these objects and between their attributes."[5] The objects themselves, or the component parts, may remain the same, but the relationships between the objects may alter, as may the relationship between the object and its environment. This is just another way of saying that changes in the relationship between the parts changes the reality of the whole. The family again will serve as an example. The family, a whole, is qualitatively and quantitatively different than its component parts, or individual systems of behavior. Rearranging the component parts as in divorce or the removal of a family member for hospitalization, military service, and so on, dramatically affects the whole. Piccard has a somewhat different focus and describes a system as "a set of dynamic general relationships which together process stimuli (inputs) through a subsystem of closer relationships, thereby producing responses (outputs)."[6] This definition stresses systems as a process rather than an entity and emphasizes its dynamic nature. Hearn, discussing the relevance of a systems perspective for social work, points out that systems

> are based on the assumption that matter, in all of its forms, living and nonliving, can be regarded as systems and that systems, as systems, have certain discrete properties that are capable of being studied. Individual, small groups ... families, organizations ... neighborhoods, and communities — in short, the entities with which social work is usually involved — can be regarded as systems with certain common properties.[7]

Analysis of these and other definitions of systems alerts us to some common elements. Whether the definitions emphasize structural or performance characteristics of systems, they share the belief that there is an interdependence and interaction between systems and that within any given system there is a high degree of organization. These assumptions provide the basic framework for the social worker's search for the patterns of activity that connect individual and societal behavior. Systems thinking focuses the professional's attention away from isolated behavioral elements and toward variables in interaction. This provides an important conceptual link for the practitioner attempting to come to grips with the complexities of human behavior and the social environment.

Prior to a discussion of special characteristics of systems the distinction between living, or organic, and non-living, or mechanical, systems needs to be made. Basic to the organic model of systems is the idea that the whole is more than the sum of its parts. That is to say the system as a totality has characteristics and activities that go beyond a simple description of the characteristics and activities of the components. It further implies that the unity of the system derives from the diverse roles and functions of the components. In non-living, or mechanistic, systems the whole is the sum of its parts. The contribution of the component parts to the whole can be simply computed. The unity of the system derives from the similarity of the component parts.

Characteristics of Systems: Boundary, Purpose, Exchange, Network

Social systems theory is predicated on the assumption that there is an interdependency between the social systems of families, groups, organizations, communities, and societies, and that within each of these components there is a high degree of internal organization. Exerting pressure on one component of the system will effect a response in another component. The slowdown of automotive production in a community has reverberations in the lives of the families dependent on employment in the automotive industry, as it does on the community that is strengthened by the automobile manufacturer's tax contribution. Just as the family, a component of the larger community system, responds to change as it occurs at the community level, so do individuals, components of the family system, react to changes occuring at the family level of organization. Understanding the interrelationship and mutual interaction between these systems of varying levels of size and complexity is the "stuff" that characterizes systems thinking. Anderson and Carter use the term *focal system* to designate the system of primary attention.[8] If the unit of analysis in the example above is the automative industry, the industry itself becomes the focal system for study. One could, however, choose a broader perspective and focus on the economic system and how it relates to prevailing political and ideological structures. Whatever the focal system identified, it is necessary to consider the relationships between various components. One way to do this, according to Hanchett, would be to identify the relationships — both potential and actual — that exist between

1. Parts of the system

2. A part of the system and the system as a whole

3. Parts of the system and parts of its environment

4. The whole system and parts of its environment

5. The whole system and its environment as a whole[9]

Relationships can exist between any or all of these discrete entities. Accurate identification of these relationship factors in the assessment phase of the helping process directs the social worker's attention to the desired target for change — whether the system as a whole, a part, or parts of the system — and helps pinpoint the type of intervention to be used. The practitioner may want to chart these relationships in such a way as to gain a clearer picture of the interaction, thereby clarifying the focus of the planned intervention.

Patterned human life is made possible through this interlocking of structured relationships that range in size from cellular to intersocietal and even cosmic levels of organization. Social workers are, however, primarily concerned with the individual, the family, the small group, the organization, the community, and the society as focal points for analysis and intervention. Whatever the size of the system, certain characteristics are manifest. The discussion that follows will focus on the characteristics of boundary, purpose, exchange, and network.

Boundary. In defining and conceptualizing systems, some authors make the distinction between *open* and *closed systems.* An open system is, according to them, constantly involved in an exchange of energy with its environment. The boundaries of an open system are permeable, allowing an interchange of materials, energy, and information with its environment. No energy exchange exists between a closed system and its environment. Energy in this context may mean a physical exchange or an ideational or informational one. Hall and Fagen suggest:

> Most organic systems are open, meaning they exchange materials, energies, or information with their environments. A system is closed if there is no import or export of energies in any of its forms such as information, heat, physical materials, etc., and therefore no change of components, an example being a chemical reaction taking place in a sealed insulated container.[10]

Stein, discussing characteristics of open and closed systems, points out that whereas living systems are open and move toward an increase in order and complexity, closed systems are characterized by increasing disorder and, eventually, disintegration.[11] When the energy flow from its environment is cut off, an open system becomes a closed one. Some severe forms of autism have been used to exemplify this point. In this condition thinking patterns become an end in themselves rather than the means to an end. The personal communication system of the autistic child is unrelated and unresponsive to external environmental forces — in this case other people. In systems terms, the boundaries of the autistic child are nonpermeable. If there is any interchange between the child and its environment, that is, other people, especially family members, it is so minimal as to serve no functional purpose. The child becomes increasingly enveloped in his or her private world, with little or no ability to engage in the family communication system. In this instance one primary intervention goal may be to open the channels of communication between system (child) and environment (family). If the child is to progress developmentally, importation of energy from the environment must be secured and maintained.

Differentiating a system from its environment is of paramount importance whether one adopts the definitions of open and closed systems presented above or not. In addressing the question of when an object belongs to a system and when it belongs to its environment, Hall and Fagen state:

> A system together with its environment makes up the universe of all things of interest in a given context. Subdivision of this universe into two sets, system and environment, can be done in many ways which are in fact quite arbitrary. Ultimately it depends on the one who is studying the particular universe as to which of the possible configurations of objects is to be taken as the system.[12]

To operationalize the task of separating system from environment the social worker must first determine essential from nonessential variables in a given context, then identify the relationships and interaction between the components. A system has components which in aggregate form the system. These components are part of one or more *subsystems*. The system, in turn, may be part of the environment of a larger system, called the *suprasystem.* A hospital's social service unit, for instance, may be analyzed as its own system made up of its own components, such as personnel, services, and users of these services. These form subsystems within the unit. However, the whole social service unit may itself be part of the subsystem of a hospital organization, which is the suprasystem. The hospital organization in turn becomes part of the larger health care system. The language of systems helps clarify the relationship between the boundaries of a system and its component parts, and the relationship between the parts themselves. In the case of the hospital social service unit one might find that tension and stress between the supervisory staff and the direct service workers in the social service unit — that is, between parts of the system — negatively affect the ability of the social service department to work cooperatively with the nursing division — that is, relationships between parts of the system and parts of the environment. These conflicts in turn directly and indirectly impact on the quality of service to individual clients.

Careful demarcation of boundaries focuses the attention of the social worker on manageable indicators and narrows the field for consideration of potential influences on the system or subsystems. These influences can be charted graphically. Chin recommends that one draw a circle, then place

> ... elements, parts, variables, inside the circle as components and draw lines through the components. The lines may be thought of as rubber bands ... which stretch on contact as the forces increase or decrease. Outside the circle is the environment, where we place all other factors which impinge upon the system.[13]

Chin's description of boundaries can be readily extrapolated to apply to the biological, psychological, and social-structural context. The biological structures of cell, organ, organ system, and organism, for example, while interdependent in function, can be isolated as separate entities for independent analysis by simple demarcation of boundaries such as skin, tissue, and membrane. Shifting the unit of attention from biological to psychological dimensions enables one to draw boundaries focusing on discrete personality traits or on the total personality system. Social-structural boundaries can be used to delimit family, political, and economic structures as well as to identify group, organization, and community variables. Religious, ideational, and value factors create cultural boundaries, and the elaborate mechanisms employed to protect these range from psychological defensiveness to the intersocietal conflict seen in war.

Summarizing boundaries, Sundberg et al. state:

> Although it is possible for us to single out an individual system for our attention, it does not exist in isolation. The world is made up of systems within systems, organizations of components each of which is organized within its own boundary. It is obvious without any theorizing that a person represents a system at one level, and the family to which he belongs, a system at another. It is also obvious that the person is an organization of many subsystems, and that there are suprasystems in which families constitute components or units.[14]

In living systems boundaries serve a regulatory function in determining the amount of energy flow (information and resources) between a system and its environment. Fig. 2.1 on page 52 presents the concept of boundaries in terms of how they open and close in response to changing environmental conditions. Representing boundaries as functioning as doors, windows, or gates illustrates the multiple purposes boundaries serve for both system maintenance and system change.

Depicting boundaries as opening and closing in response to varying conditions in the external environment suggests that boundaries themselves are fluid and flexible rather than rigid. The boundaries of a given system need to be open enough to respond to changing environmental conditions — to incorporate new energy and information — yet be firm enough to maintain the internal integrity of the system. Hanchett points out that one of the primary indicators of the health of a given community is the flexibility of its institutional boundaries.[15] She suggests that the health planner consider the internal and external pressures that create troublesome boundaries as part of the process of assessing the health needs of a given community.

Before leaving the subject of boundaries it is important to point out that living systems with open and flexible boundaries not only incorporate information and energy from the environment but process this energy so it is assimilated into the identity of the new system. Systems that are inflexible and cannot import energy from the environment gradually die.

Purpose. Chapter 4 deals specifically with goal-directed behavior and life tasks. It is our intention here to discuss purpose as one characteristic of systems and to relate purpose to the biological, psychological, social-structural, and cultural dimensions of behavior.

In order for a system to achieve its goals balance must be maintained both within the components of the system and with the environmental forces interacting with it. The concept of *homeostasis* refers to the property of systems that assures continued stability between the various system components. *Equilibrium* is a term often used interchangeably with homeostasis. Both terms refer to the regulatory processes through which the system achieves a state of internal and external balance. Critics of the concept of homeostasis argue that it is essentially a conservative concept through which maintenance of the status quo becomes the primary motivational force of the system. Perpetuation of archaic welfare policies, for example, assures the continuation of the welfare bureaucracy with seemingly little concern for the well-being of the consumer. The current trend in both private and public agencies of maintaining a balanced budget may be at the expense of the recipients of service. Equilibrium is maintained, but it can hardly be described as a desired state. Anderson and Carter borrow the term "steady state" from physics to denote the condition in which the system is "maintaining a viable relationship with its environment and its components."[16] They argue against a static and fixed concept of balance and formulate a presentation in which system change and system maintenance are seen as motivational correlates. In a similar vein Brill points out:

> ... It is obvious that there are elements that strive to maintain the status quo as well as those which are orientated toward activity and change. These divergent tendencies are related to the two basic functions of a system: (1) its internal task to maintain the balanced relationship among the parts of which it is composed; and (2) its external task to perform the function for which it was devised and to relate to its environment.[17]

A view of purpose that directs the system to seek change and new experience as well as stability is compatible with professional purpose as presented in this text. It is also consistent with the concept of an open system with fluid and flexible boundaries. The implication of this to psychological and sociological theories will be suggested later.

Purpose is dramatically evidenced at the biological level through the infinite adaptive arrangements on which the continuation of the species is predicated. The progressive increase in complexity seen in biological systems illustrates the organism's simultaneous concern for survival and change. Maintaining the integrity of a system is, in and of itself, not enough; growth and evolution of new and emerging forms is also a characteristic of human life.

Extending the biological metaphor further, Sundberg et al. add:

> ... behavior is often a component of the physiological homeostatic processes themselves. The act of folding one's arms, drawing one's body into a compact ball, or even getting out of bed to find an extra blanket are part of the process by which constant temperature is maintained.[18]

Menninger applies the concept of homeostasis to the psychological dimension of behavior and also emphasizes the motivational pulls toward stability and change that direct goal-seeking behavior:

> It would be one-sided indeed to ignore the fact that there are other determinants of human behavior than merely passive adjustment to it. There is a strong urge within the organism to effect change, to initiate some of the very disturbances which the regulatory processes of the organism are patterned to resist. It is the conflict between the wish for change — newness, variety, opportunity — and the fear of other consequences of change which makes for the complexity of human behavior.[19]

Psychological theories acknowledging change and growth as motivational forces underlying behavior offer more promise to the profession of social work than restrictive psychologies which emphasize adjustment as adaptation. The individual is not a passive reactor to environmental forces but an active participant in shaping his or her environment. Clarke-Stewart's work on the interactive nature of parenting exemplifies this point.[20]

Social-structural explanations of behavior focusing on homeo-stasis have been targets of criticism by conflict theorists. The point of contention is that they are inherently conservative arguments in which preservation of the status quo becomes the *sine qua non* of the system's purpose. Uncritical application of biological concepts to social-structural phenomena, as in the Social Darwinism of the nineteenth century or in some of the more recent developments in sociobiology, has profound implications for the welfare of human-kind. In both instances scientific data is used to support political ideologies. Social-structural theories stressing growth and change are more closely aligned to the professional purpose of social work.

Attitudes, ideas, and values related to such fundamental human concerns as family life, sex role identification, the meaning of work, and the existence (or nonexistence) of the deity form the nucleus around which cultural purposes are organized. A shared sense of pur-pose solidifies cultural boundaries, and much human effort Is ex-pended toward both maintaining and changing cultural goals.

This is not to suggest that purpose in the sense of goal achieve-ment is the primary motivating force in determining the behavioral direction of the organism. A study of organizational structures and dynamics often points out the tendency of many organizations to continue to function long after their original purpose has been achieved. Purpose in such a context becomes equated with survival and new organizational-environmental alliances are negotiated to per-petuate the organization's life. Gilbert, Miller, and Specht point out that the relationship between organizational survival and goal achievement is not necessarily a compatible one. Their warning is particularly directed to reform-oriented organizations in which en-vironmental forces have a vested interest in preserving the status quo.

> ... Until they have the strength to withstand assault by agencies that are the targets of their reform efforts, reform-oriented organizations must behave in ways that will not evoke strong opposition from the environment.[21]

The history of the Economic Opportunity Act, specifically with its early emphasis on grass roots community organization, exemplifies the very real dilemmas that often occur when various populations have different ideas of the system's purpose. Religious groups, feminist organizations, and consumers or potential consumers of service may have contradictory beliefs and ideas about a general hospital providing abortion on demand. The social work practitioner, as part of the assessment phase of the intervention process, needs to be alerted to this kind of congruence or lack of congruence between the components of a system in perceiving the purpose of the system or its component parts.

Purpose in the context used above serves as one of the variables around which a system organizes its energy and draws its boundaries. We will now focus on two related systems characteristics, exchange and networks.

Exchange. The boundaries of a system, which establish the system's integrity, are usually permeable — that is, they are open to new sources of energy and information from the environment. Fig-

FIGURE 2.1[22]

Visualizing System Boundaries

In Living Systems,

Boundaries
Function

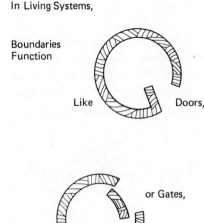

Like   Doors,

Windows,

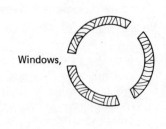

or Gates,

Responding to Different Conditions
of the Organism, Its Environment,
and the Interaction Between Them
at Any One Point in Time.

ure 2.1 shows how boundaries open and close in response to elements within the organism and relationships between the organism
and its environment. The term *exchange* as used in this discussion
refers to the process of interaction between the system and its environment.

Hanchett's diagram (figure 2.1) raises interesting questions
about the exchange between a given system and its environment.
Can a living system completely shut out all energy, information, and
resources from its environment without dying? Consistent with our
previous discussion on open and closed systems, it is our contention that no such entity as a completely closed system exists.

When the boundary between a system and its environment is
characterized by a door, the health of the system may be in jeopardy. If the boundaries between a system and its environment have
gates and windows which allow for fluidity and flexibility, the exchange maximizes the growth potential of the system. When the
door is open so wide that the system is flooded with new ener-
gies, resources, or information the system runs the risk of losing its
identity. The door, then, must be open wide enough to assure importation of energy from the system's environment, yet not so wide
as to become engulfed in the identity of another system. The door,
window, and gate analogy can be visually represented along the
continuum of open-closed systems discussed earlier. (See figure
2.2).

FIGURE 2.2

Hanchett's Analogy Presented on a Continuum of Open-Closed Systems.

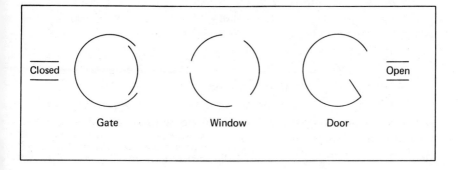

Closed   Gate   Window   Door   Open

Living systems require resources in order to function effectively and achieve their purposes. Resources may be supplied from within the system or from the external environment. These internal or external resources may be thought of as *inputs*; once *processed* by the system, they produce *outputs*. In the biological process of breathing the organism receives oxygen (input) from the environment and discharges carbon dioxide (output). The biological process of eating further illustrates this point — the body processes food (input) and discharges waste (output). Psychological parallels can also be found. Parental attitudes (input) are significant variables in the infant's developing a sense of security (output). Inputs can be real or imagined. If the individual interprets a situation as real (input), it will produce real behavioral consequences (output). This is what is meant by the self-fulfilling prophecy — the individual behaves in a way consistent with his or her interpretation of an event. An adolescent, for instance, may feel overly conscious of bodily weight when in fact he or she falls well within the average weight range for his or her age group. Here the cultural values regarding desirable appearance (input) have been internalized and are manifest in the individual's body image (output).

Social-structural exchanges can be conceptualized in terms of the reciprocal relationships occuring between individual (or family) systems and political, economic, and ideological systems. Bell and Vogel's conception of these as functional interchanges is represented in figure 2.3.[23] These exchanges may be concete, as in labor (input) in exchange for wages (output), or behavioral, as in the nuclear family's knowledge of community standards (input) in exchange for the assurance of individual and familial identity (output). Systems process inputs in order to produce results, or outputs. For example, cultural values and beliefs (input) are internalized, or processed by the individual. This processing by a component of the system — in this example, an individual — is the system's own way of digesting information with the goal of using it to serve the needs of both the component and the suprasystem.

Examination of functional interchanges between and across boundaries aids the social worker in developing a dynamic interpretation of events and phenomena. It can also be used as a tool to explain interchanges between political and economic systems, as

FIGURE 2.3

The Interchanges Between the Nuclear Family and the Functional Subsystems of Society

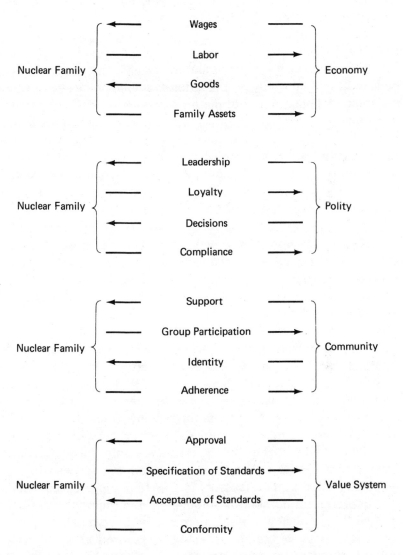

Norman W. Bell and Ezra F. Vogel, eds., *A Modern Introduction to the Family*, rev. ed. (New York: The Free Press, 1968).

well as to explain relationships among family members. For example, a planning agency may be interested in assessing the potential impact of a proposed industrial complex on the economic life of a community, while a social worker studying the same phenomena in another setting may focus on the effect such a development will have on community housing patterns. The relationship between these political and economic decisions impact on such internal family activities as division of labor and the establishment of patterns of leadership and authority. In the latter example, political and economic systems become part of the environment of the family system. In the former example, the family is viewed as a part of the subsystem of larger political and economic systems. Shifting the focus of the interaction between the nuclear family and the various systems of influence as presented in figure 2.3 to the interaction between the systems themselves (economy, polity, community, and value system) will help explain the idea of networks.

Network. *Networks* have been described as "aggregations of connecting lines, links, or channels."[24] They result from the exchanges described in the preceding sections. In some instances a network is a system in itself. The social welfare system, for instance, is a network of interrelated agencies and services; kinship systems are networks of related roles and relationships. Exchanges are made within and between systems. When a system of patterned relationships develops, a network is established.

Any given system, which we will call system A, obtains input from other systems, which we will call systems B and C. Inputs for system A are, therefore, outputs for systems B and C. To look at a more concrete example, the family system (system A) is dependent on input in the form of economic resources from the economic system (system B) and in the form of educational services from the public education system (system C). The family processes these inputs to produce a number of outputs. Among them are such things as food and housing for its members and youngsters properly nourished, motivated, and intellectually prepared to attend school. These outputs of the family system then become inputs to individual family members, who are biological systems, as well as to the economic and educational systems. Any output has an *impact*, or an effect, on the system which uses it as an input. To continue the above example, if children are not adequately nourished their growth and behavior will be seriously affected. In addition, children who are not prepared for school by the family pose a task for the educational system that is altogether different than if the children are prepared.

We can see, then, that the input, output, impact experience of each system becomes enmeshed in networks of interdependence that relate to the input, output, and impact of other systems. In other words, within the suprasystem are networks of systems that impact on each other through the exchange of inputs and outputs. This is why behavior cannot be looked at out of context. It exists as part of a system which is in turn part of a network of systems. To adequately understand behavior, one has to place it within this larger context. The social problems of racism, sexism, ageism, and homophobia* serve as examples. They are deeply rooted cultural components which affect the social-structural arrangements through which goods and services are allocated. For instance, forcing the elderly out of the work force condemns many of them to poverty and accelerated physical and mental deterioration through the interaction of the economic, political, and family systems. These complex problems are created and perpetuated through system networks and cry for systemic rather than individual resolution. Those offering professional help need to be aware of these networks in order to select appropriate kinds of intervention.

Social workers deal with many types of systems. Among the most commonly encountered are individual, family, community, economic, political, educational, medical, and social welfare organizational systems. Each system has its own distinctive characteristics. To illustrate, each family has a unique pattern of relationships among its members and with the other systems with which it interacts. Similarly, social welfare agencies have distinctive internal structures as well as established relationships with other systems. Certain system networks are more common than others. A social

---

*Homophobia is the fear of homosexuality. Like any prejudice, it is not based in fact and it often leads to discriminatory behavior, in this case against homosexuals.

FIGURE 2.4

Illustrations of System Characteristics

Dimensions of Behavior and Selected Systems

System Characteristics

	Boundary	Purpose	Exchange	Network
Biological				
Cell	Skin	Survival	Input (oxygen)	Caregiving in the family affects access to life-sustaining resources;
Organ	Membrane	Adaptation	Process (breathing)	Industrial pollution affects the quality of the physical environment; the survival of the organism affects family life and the work force.
Organ system	Body		Output (carbon dioxide)	
Psychological				
Person	Self/other	Change/growth	Input (stimulus)	Caregiving in the family affects self-identity;
		Identity	Process (internalization)	Societal definitions of desirable characteristics affect relations with others and ability to fit into societal structures.
			Output (response behavior)	

Social-structural		Stability/change	Input (community)	Subculture values affect formation of social structures; existing social structures control individual behavior;
Political	Party			
Economic	Class structure		Process (adherence to norms)	Individual behavior can challenge values.
			Output (group identity)	
Cultural				
Ideological	Ethnic groupings	Group identity	Input (values/beliefs)	Technology affects quality of life; values affect development and use of technology;
	Religious	Cohesion	Process (internalization)	Technology affects biological survival.
Value framework			Output (solidarity)	

work agency, for example, usually interacts with some social welfare agencies more than others. Social workers need to understand these established networks, since they have great significance for the agency's inputs and outputs. People giving professional help should also be alert to new networks that can be established to offer other needed inputs or more effectively use the agency's outputs.

Summary

The preceding material discusses the system characteristics of boundary, purpose, exchange, and network as related to the biological, psychological, social-structural, and cultural dimensions of behavior. It underlines selected ideas and concepts that, rooted in professional purpose, influence the integration of individual and societal aspects of behavior. Some of these ideas are graphically presented in figure 2.4.

Since systems ideas are essentially abstractions, the language of systems often obscures the information it is intended to convey. However, these ideas and concepts provide a framework for viewing the individual, group, or community, not simply as a passive reactor to environmental forces, but as an agent that is, at the same time, molding and shaping the environment. It is this simultaneous dual focus on person and environment that enriches our understanding of professional purpose.

Successful intervention at the *interface*, or point of connection, between individuals and social institutions is predicated on such a dual focus. Systems thinking helps clarify interactions at this interface by providing us with a set of tools through which the interactions can be visually represented. Boundary, purpose, exchange, and network are some of the tools. We are not suggesting they make up a complete kit, simply that understanding these properties can help us deal with the vast amount of biological, social, and behavioral science data available to the practitioner.

Whereas systems share both structural and performance characteristics discussed in this chapter, any given system is made up of a unique set of people with unique boundaries, purposes, exchanges, and networks. Chapter 3 will focus on the concept of human diversity and develop a perspective to help us understand its role as a behavioral determinant.

Study Questions

1. The profession of social work has evidenced a dual tradition of individualized treatment and social reform. How does systems thinking provide a conceptual base to make this dichotomy unnecessary?

2. A systems approach posits that change introduced in one part of the system effects change in other parts of the system. What is the implication of this assumption for the social worker's task of directing changes?

3. Systems theory, or selected ideas and concepts implicit in it, can be easily represented graphically. Make a diagram in which your class is viewed as a social system — illustrate its boundaries, then chart its relationship to the various suprasystems of which it is a part and the subsystems that constitute its components.

4. Societal resources are allocated through social-structural arrangements encompassing political, economic, and ideational systems. How does the interrelationship of these systems impact on the public social policy of income maintenance? Health care? The role and status of women and minorities?

5. Many argue that racism, sexism, ageism, and homophobia are deeply ingrained in our present institutional arrangements. Design a social work response to those issues using a systems perspective.

Notes

1.   D. H. Lawrence, *Apocalypse* (New York: The Viking Press, 1932).

2.   Gerald Egan and Michael A. Cowan, *People in Systems: A Model for*

Development in the Human Service Professions and Education (Monterey, Ca.: Brooks/Cole Publishing Company, 1979), p. 6.

3. Egan and Cowan, p. 6.

4. Ludwig von Bertalanffy, "General Systems Theory," in *General Systems Yearbook for the Society for General Research*, von Bertalanffy, ed., vol. 1 (Bedford, Mass.: Society for General Systems Research, 1956), pp. 1–10.

5. A. D. Hall and R. E. Fagen, "Definition of System" in *Modern Systems Research for the Behavioral Scientist*, Walter Buckley, ed. (Chicago: Aldine Publishing Company, 1968), p. 81.

6. Betty Piccard, *An Introduction to Social Work: A Primer*, rev. ed. (Homewood, Ill.: Dorsey Press, 1979), p. 14.

7. Gordon Hearn, ed., *The General Systems Approach: Contribution Toward an Holistic Conception of Social Work*, (New York: Council on Social Work Education, 1969), p. 2.

8. Ralph E. Anderson and Irl Carter, *Human Behavior in the Social Environment: A Social Systems Approach*, 2nd ed. (New York: Aldine Publishing Co., 1978), p. 11.

9. Effie Hanchett, *Community Health Assessment: A Conceptual Tool Kit* (New York: John Wiley and Sons, 1979), p. 24.

10. Hall and Fagen, p. 83.

11. Irma Stein, *Systems Theory, Science, and Social Work* (Metuchen, New Jersey: Scarecrow Press, 1974), p. 12.

12. Hall and Fagen, p. 83.

13. Robert Chin, "The Utility of Systems Models and Developmental Models for Practitioners," in *The Planning of Change: Readings in the Applied Behavioral Sciences*, Warren G. Bennis et al., eds. (New York: Holt, Rinehart, and Winston, 1961), p. 201.

14. Norman D. Sundberg, Leona E. Tyler, and Julian R. Taplin, *Clinical Psychology: Expanding Horizons*, 2nd ed. (New York: Appelton-Century-Crofts, 1973), p. 100.

15 Hanchett, p. 80.

16. Anderson and Carter, p. 22.

17. Naomi Brill, *Working with People: The Helping Process*, 2nd ed. (Philadelphia: J. B. Lippincott Company, 1978), p. 83.

18. Sundberg, Tyler, Taplin, p. 97.

19.   Karl Menninger, *The Vital Balance: The Life Process in Mental Health and Illness* (New York: The Viking Press, 1963), p. 85.

20.   Alison Clarke-Stewart, *Child Care in the Family* (New York: Academic Press, 1977).

21.   Neil Gilbert, Henry Miller, and Harry Specht, *An Introduction to Social Work Practice* (Englewood Cliffs, N. J.: Prentice-Hall, 1980), p. 190.

22.   Hanchett, p. 81.

23.   Norman W. Bell and Ezra F. Vogel, eds., *A Modern Introduction to the Family*, rev. ed. (New York: The Free Press, 1968), p. 10.

24.   Hanchett, p. 72.

Additional Readings

Barker, R. *Habitats, Environments, and Human Behavior.* San Francisco: Jossey-Bass, 1978.

Bennis, Warren G.; Benne, Kenneth D.; Chin, Robert; and Corey, Kenneth E., eds. *The Planning of Change.* 3rd ed. New York: Holt, Rinehart and Winston, 1976.

Buckley, Walter. *Sociology and Modern Systems Theory.* Englewood Cliffs, N. J.: Prentice-Hall, 1967.

Etzioni, Amitai. *Modern Organizations.* Englewood Cliffs, N. J.: Prentice-Hall, 1964.

Laszlo, E. *The Systems View of the World.* New York: Braziller, 1974.

Litterer, Joseph, ed. *Organizations: Systems, Control and Adaptation.* Vol. 2. 2nd ed. New York: John Wiley, 1969.

Miller, James. "Living Systems: Basic Concepts," *Behavioral Science* 10 (1965): 193–237.

Parsons, Talcott, *The Social System.* New York: Free Press, 1964.

Pincus, A. and Minahan, Anne. *Social Work Practice: Model and Method.* Itasca, Ill.: F. E. Peacock Publishers, 1973.

Rothman, Jack; Erlich, John L.; and Teresa, Joseph G. *Promoting Innovation and Change in Organizations and Communities.* New York: John Wiley, 1976.

Werley, Harriet; Zorich, Ann; Zajkowski, Myron; and Zagornik, A. Daron, eds. *Health Research: A Systems Approach.* New York: Springer, 1976.

In a long term evolutionary perspective, diversity is the finest insurance policy available to any species. It follows from this perspective that any great reduction in biological or cultural diversity diminishes mankind, not only esthetically, but practically in terms of survival of the species. Cultural plurality is not only a desirable social goal, but a biological necessity.

*Jane H. Underwood**

CHAPTER 3

Human Diversity and Human Needs

*Jane H. Underwood, *Biocultural Interactions and Human Variation* (Dubugue, Iowa, William C. Brown, Co., 1975), p. 64.

Introduction

This chapter will focus in detail on human diversity. In chapter 1 we saw how human diversity can be used to create a framework for understanding human behavior in conjunction with the ideas of systems and purposeful behavior. First the idea of human diversity will be defined and elaborated. Then the ways in which human diversity affects the identification and pursuit of human needs will be analyzed. This will be followed by a systematic review of the biological, psychological, social-structural, and cultural concepts basic for understanding human diversity. The interrelationships among these multiple concepts, taken from a range of social, biological, and behavioral science disciplines, become apparent when organized around the idea of human diversity. Introduced in this chapter, the application of the idea of human diversity to specific human behavior situations will be further developed in a later chapter.

In chapter 2 the idea of systems was discussed at length. This chapter enriches and extends that discussion. Human diversity cuts across various systems and helps explain why parts of systems relate as they do. For example, the ways in which the family relates to the work place (two systems that are part of the larger social-structural system) are very much affected by the cultural beliefs shared by family members (which may result from a shared ethnic heritage) as well as by the characteristics of individual family members (such as age or physical disabilities). In other words, the characteristics of the people who make up a system affect the operation of that system. The ways in which a system is perceived and experienced by its members are also affected by the characteristics of the people and the system. As will be seen in the next chapter, human diversity is also important for understanding why people pursue their life goals and life activities as they do.

The Meaning of Human Diversity

Human diversity refers to the ways in which people are different. As we will see in more detail later in this chapter, the sources of differences among people are biological (genetically established age, sex, race, and physical characteristics), psychological (personality and perception), social-structural (ethnicity, gender, socioeconomic standing, and sexual preference), and cultural (idea systems, language, and technology). These characteristics are used to group people together. Such grouping affects people's self-identity and the way they are treated by others. It is for this reason that human diversity is so important — it strongly affects people's life styles and life chances. This is also why social work professionals need to be concerned with human diversity — it affects people's life styles and has an influence on why people do what they do. Its effects on people's life chances influence their needs as well as the helping strategies that are most likely to successfully meet those needs.

Human diversity is a complex idea that cuts across many individual social, biological, and behavioral science disciplines. Biology, sociology, psychology, economics, political science, and anthropology are especially relevant to the study of human diversity, since concepts from these disciplines are used to describe and explain how and why differences between people occur. We cannot emphasize too strongly the importance of understanding these differences in developing the ability to comprehend the realities of people's lives. Only when these realities are grasped can reasonable efforts be made to help them live more meaningful and rewarding lives.[1] Figure 3.1 provides an overview of the four sources of human diversity, along with a summary of the major subcategories of each of these sources. The rest of this chapter will be devoted to describing these sources and subcategories in more detail.

Each person obviously possesses several characteristics simultaneously — for example, age, sex, race, personality, socioeconomic standing, sexual preference, and language. How, then, are we to understand how people get allocated to groups and disentangle which group has the most influence on a person's behavior at any particular time? We can do so by understanding the criteria used by society in allocating importance to various sources and types of diversity, and by understanding that specific types of diversity may be defined as especially important in certain situations. For example, in the United States race is very important and very pervasive — peo-

FIGURE 3.1

The Four Sources of Human Diversity and Their Major Subcategories

Source	Subcategory
Biological	Genetic Inheritance (Obtained from parents, grandparents, and the larger breeding population; combined in a unique way for each individual; strongly influenced by environmental conditions)
Psychological	Personality (Distinctive way individual uses information to meet needs under specific environmental conditions) Perception and Cognition (Distinctive way individual perceives and processes information; strong biological component)
Social-structural	Age (Biological capacity and social expectations) Sex/Gender (Biological capacity and social expectations) Ethnicity (Cultural characteristics and social expectations) Physical Characteristics (Disabilities, appearance, and social expectations associated with each) Socioeconomic Standing (Access to societal resources; influence on life chances and life styles; societal expectations) Religion (Cultural characteristics and social expectations) Sexual Preference (Homosexuality/ Heterosexuality) (Cultural characteristics and social expectations)
Cultural	Dominant Culture (Values and norms that characterize a large societal group) Subcultures (Smaller distinctive cultural groups existing within a dominant culture)

ple are routinely assessed and processed according to their race. Indeed, race is so important that it is often used to refer to nonracial characteristics such as ethnicity (Germans, Poles, and Italians are members of the same race but different ethnic groups) and religion (Jews share a religion and ethnic characteristics derived from it rather than a race). On the other hand, age may be relatively unimportant as a distinguishing characteristic except at the two ends of the age continuum (under 18 and over 65, for example) or in specific situations (such as applying for a job).

Obviously, then, the *importance* of human diversity is socially determined, although the diversity itself may be biologically and/or socially determined. The criteria used to group people, and the importance of those groupings, are created by society. Once they exist, however, they become important parts of the social reality in that society. An excellent example of this process is provided by developmentally disabled children, who have traditionally been misunderstood and therefore mistreated by the public school system. Because their needs *and abilities* have not been properly understood, they have often been considered disruptive in the classroom and hence were shunted off to "special classes" with the following results:

> When children were considered "different," public schools refused to acknowledge their rights to an equal opportunity to learn. By placing all impaired children in the same setting — often referred to as a "dumping ground" — schools projected a twofold but contradictory message: (1) such children were deviant or different from most children and (2) their individual needs could all be met in the same way.[2]

Society's definition of criteria for differentiating between groups has two sources. One is the *societal* definition imposed on people who share a certain characteristic, such as age or sex. The other is the definition of self which *emerges from within the group itself.* The combination of these two sources has been described as the *dual perspective* on diversity.[3] It is a critical idea for understanding human diversity since it allows us to see how the two definitions may be different. For example, United States society has tended to define homosexuals as deviant and "sick." Members of this group have challenged this definition by developing their own support groups,[4] doing research to refute the data used by others to stigmatize them,[5] and publicly disseminating information that explains and supports their own self-definition.[6]

To adequately understand members of a diverse group, then, one has to understand *common human needs* in addition to each member's distinctive needs. At first it may seem paradoxical to talk about common human needs along with diverse needs, though the two ideas are actually intertwined. All members of the human species share certain life tasks around which we organize our need-meeting behavior. We all seek to meet the *same needs* but do so in many *different ways*. We all must eat to survive, but some people hunt, some fish, some plant, some shop at food stores, and some do all of these things. We all need a sense of security and identity, but in some groups this results from cooperation while in others it results from competition. Also, the level at which needs are met vary. In some groups, for example, eating very selectively and in moderation is considered desirable, while in others eating great amounts is preferred. Finally, the environment strongly affects a group's ability, as well as its methods, to meet needs. And so we have come full circle. As humans, we all share a set of common needs for which the group we belong to defines appropriate need-meeting strategies. These group memberships and definitions then become the basis for our interaction with the environment and hence our ability to meet our needs. In other words, the groups to which we belong, and which are based on diversity, affect how we try to meet our needs as well as how others respond to our efforts. The basic needs themselves are essentially common to all groups. As Goldschmidt notes, "Just as studies of animal structure and function have shown that a variety of biological solutions are possible for a given environmental problem, so too a variety of social solutions may be utilized in meeting common human predicaments."[7]

What are these basic common human needs? There is a remarkable degree of agreement among social, biological, and behavioral scientists about these needs. Abraham Maslow's formulation is well known. He lists physiological needs (such as condition of the blood, the body's chemical balance, sensory functioning, and hormonal functioning), safety needs (security, stability, freedom from fear and anxiety, need for structure, and so forth), belongingness and love needs (such as affectionate relationships, feeling "rooted," and not feeling rejected), esteem needs (self-respect, self-esteem, sense of mastery, a sound reputation, and so forth), and self-actualization ("... becoming everything that one is capable of becoming").[8] Forgus and Shulman list the following common human needs:

... Nourishment and contact, protection or safety, mastery, and sensory variation. Nourishment, contact, and protection are concerned with bodily growth and survival. Mastery is concerned with effective manipulation of the environment. Sensory variation is necessary for innate programs to be aroused and perceptual systems to develop.[9]

Horney lists six needs: emotional warmth, security, freedom, good will, guidance, and healthy friction.[10] Finally, Charlotte Towle's classic formulation of common human needs lists physical welfare and personality development, emotional growth and development of intellectual capacity, relationship with others, and spiritual needs.[11]

All of these formulations of basic needs include physical needs, relationship needs, feelings of competence, and some sense of well-being. Obviously each of these needs can be elaborated in many ways, and diverse groups do this. Definitions of healthful nutritional levels, preferred physical appearance, customary types of social relationships, indicators of competent behavior, and desirable life patterns are all ways particular groups adapt common human needs to themselves. In Puerto Rico, for example, many people feel that preserving the natural beauty and cleanliness of the beaches is preferable to environmentally destructive industrial development even though industry might create jobs and raise income levels.[12] In this example, acceptable levels at which physical needs are met might be lower than in other societies, but the Puerto Rican sense of physical well-being would be increased with access to natural resources like the beach and the ocean. Other ethnic groups might choose to meet this need in an entirely different manner. Though ways of meeting needs vary, no way is inherently better or worse than any other.

In addition to looking at ways diverse groups meet needs, one must also look at the way needs are prioritized. Maslow has hypothesized a need hierarchy, saying that needs will be met starting with physiological needs and moving up through self-actualization needs.[13] Unless lower order needs are met, higher order needs will not be attended to, a concept of need prioritizing shared by Freud, Erikson, and Jung, among others.[14] A human diversity perspective raises questions about such an invariant prioritizing of needs, however. Many ethnic groups will sacrifice some level of physiological and safety needs in order to achieve relationship and well-being needs, for example. A dramatic example has been the sacrifices in living conditions and living standards made by Southeast Asian immigrants to the United States who, rather than improving their own living standard, use resources to protect kin and ethnic ties so essential to their sense of identity and belonging.[15] Other ethnic groups have done the same, as have such diverse groups as abused women, homosexuals, and elderly people when banding together in attempts to achieve the greatest good for the greatest number. Here again the interplay of individual and social needs is illustrated.

Understanding needs requires an awareness of common needs that essentially derive from the characteristics of humans as a species as well as the way these needs become defined, elaborated, and prioritized by diverse groups. Set formulations of need hierarchies should be approached with caution, since different groups may develop their own ranking of needs (although the needs themselves may be similar). Hierarchies may also blind one to the fact that people are meeting many needs at once. Indeed, we struggle with all of our needs throughout our lifetime although the resources available to us for meeting various needs may change over time, a topic to be discussed at more length in chapter 5. This makes it very difficult to speak of clear hierarchies of needs except in a very general sense. Instead, we see that needs interact in very complex ways and give rise to equally complex patterns of need-meeting behavior.

Helping professionals must be especially sensitive when attempting to understand the needs of those with whom they work. Needs must be mutually explored, defined, and prioritized — tasks for which using the dual perspective is essential. Care must be taken to avoid imposing concepts of "normal" needs and "normal" need-meeting strategies. People must be free to define and prioritize needs for themselves. Strategies selected by people for themselves must not be seen as "deviant," although if they create problems in the balance between individual and social needs, the implications of these problems must be explored. Common human needs is a concept which sensitizes helping professionals to areas of social functioning which may be problematic for everyone. However, these needs mean different things and are managed differently by members of diverse groups. Understanding these differences provides the most secure foundation for finding ways to help diverse groups of people use more effectively the institutions of society.

Sources of Human Diversity: Biological

The most basic source of human difference is the genetic uniqueness provided by the individual's *genotype*, or the information encoded in an embryo's set of genes.[16] Genes come from each parent and each grandparent as well as the larger population from which the parents are drawn, called a *breeding population*.[17] In addition to representing a variety of sources, each person's genes are combined in a unique pattern which ensures the uniqueness of each individual.[18] Human diversity, then, results fundamentally from this range of genetic sources as well as the way in which genes are combined.

Actually, genetics accounts for both diversity and continuity. While the individual is unique in his or her particular combination of genes, all genes, except for mutant genes, come from somewhere in the breeding population and most often from the immediate kin network. This is why race and ethnicity have been thought to be such important determinants of behavior. To the degree that an ethnic group inhabits a particular geographic area — often defined by national boundaries such as Italy, Thailand, Chile, and so forth — its members are likely to form a breeding population.[19] This increases the likelihood that members of the group will share certain physical characteristics such as hair color, complexion, and susceptibility to disease.[20] Similar factors apply to racial groups if, through tradition or social segregation, they are confined to particular geographical areas or their members may only mate with each other.[21]

Increasingly, geographical and social boundaries are being crossed so that there is far more intermixing of breeding populations. This provides another illustration of the way biological and social factors interact since nowadays boundaries are being crossed by technology, such as airplanes, and social policies, such as immigration policies. This increases the range of genetic possibilities for each individual and creates a greater range of physical characteristics in the population as a whole. This increasing physical diversity is a biological fact rather than something desirable or undesirable. Unless physical characteristics strongly influence behavior — a topic to be discussed at greater length later — their importance will be socially defined rather than biologically determined. For example, there is little evidence to support genetic differences in intelligence among racial groups.[22] However, if racial groups are treated as if there are such differences there will be real consequences associated with membership in a particular racial group. Indeed, differential treatment may even lead to differences in intelligence because of limited access to resources for developing potential intelligence.[23] These are all *social* forces though, and have relatively little to do with genetics.

The interplay of social and genetic factors is of critical importance to biological development in other ways as well. All of them affect human diversity. Mazur and Robertson note:

> The genes contain directions for the building of cells, organs, and organ systems and sets limits on their growth and function. The effects of genes on behavior are indirect, being accomplished through the constructed biological attributes. The day-to-day functioning of these biological attributes is not just a consequence of genetic instruction. . . . They also depend on stimuli from the physical and social environment.[24]

Because humans have rather limited instinctual behavior, they depend instead on social stimulation to learn how to act within the limits set by their genes. In other words, in humans genes establish *potentials* rather than unmodifiable *programs* of behavior.[25] The human organism does appear to have periods during which particular potentials are maximally attained. For example, as Mazur and Robertson state, "the organism must reach a certain minimal state of neurological development before it can begin to develop language."[26] On the other hand, if the necessary environmental stimulation does not occur during the period of biological readiness, the capacity to perform a particular activity may be greatly decreased.[27] Later, when psychological factors in human diversity are discussed, we will see that *the kind* of environmental stimulation is as important for future development as whether or not it exists at all.

A second type of interaction between biological and social factors is the effect of physical care on human development. This interaction is most clearly seen during pregnancy when the actions of the mother can have serious consequences for the fetus. As Underwood notes, "Genetic action does not occur in a vacuum. The action of any gene involves the effects of other genes, beginning from the instant of fertilization (inter-genic action) and extending to include the effects of the maternal environment (fetal-maternal interactions) and a whole range of internal (bodily) and external (extra-somatic) influences which we experience throughout the course of our lives."[28] Nutrition is critical to the normal physical development of the fetus as well as for a minimum-risk delivery. Substance abuse, such as the use of drugs and alcohol, can also affect fetal development, including the birth of an addicted infant. The age of the parents and the quality of prenatal care the mother receives can also affect fetal development, as can the kind of medication the mother takes. (Birth defects have been associated with a number of relatively common medications, including the tragic experiences with Thalidomide.) While proper nutrition and medical care are critically important for the fetus, they are also important during infancy and childhood. Nurturance and physical protection are also significant social factors affecting biological development during these periods.

Throughout the life span the interplay between social and biological factors continues. Accidents may occur at any time, having drastic effects on physical functioning. Illness may strike and cause permanent damage to the biological organism. In old age, withdrawal from social activities may accelerate physiological deterioration and increase physical dependency. We are now having to understand and make responsible decisions about genetic engineering.[29] The ability to decide what kind of genes are desirable and to create life artificially have opened up potentials of many kinds. On one hand, this may make it possble to eliminate genetically created illness and disability. On the other hand, human diversity as it is presently created by genetic inheritance can potentially be destroyed. The results of genetic engineering are in part unknown, but opportunities exist for population control which could be destructive.

In summarizing the biological factors influencing human diversity, we must take note of a number of critical points. Each individual starts with a unique biochemical structure. The development of this structure occurs within limits set by the organism's genetic composition. Within those limits social factors strongly influence development and create situations to determine the levels at which biological potentials are achieved. Human diversity, then, begins with genetic individuality and further develops through the interaction of the physical organism with its environment. Diverse characteristics such as age, sex, race, ethnicity, physical ability, physical appearance, personality characteristics, and intelligence all have a biological component. How they influence people's lives, however, depends on social definitions and social structuring of behavior, giving rise to such questions as are the elderly respected? are women given equal opportunity in the job market? are the handicapped defined as useless burdens? are blonds expected to have more fun?

Our understanding of biological functioning is at the same time sophisticated and poorly developed. We understand a great deal about the functioning of physiological organs and even the whole biological system, yet we do not know a great deal about the biological basis of *social* behavior. We know that drugs affect behavior, yet do not understand how their effects are modified by different personalities and different situations. We know that people with different physical characteristics (pretty, big, handicapped, active, and so forth) are treated differently, but we don't yet know the complex interaction between these variables. We know that there is probably some genetic basis for schizophrenia, introversion/extroversion, and aggression, but do not understand well the interaction between genes and the environment with respect to these behaviors. We know that there is a relationship between hormone functioning, stress, and illness, but its exact structure is unclear. There is reason to believe that there is a biological basis for sexual preference, but the interplay of biological and social factors leading to sexual identity and sexual preference are still being studied. In conclusion, then, we can only say that biology strongly affects human diversity in a multitude of ways, only some of which are understood at the present time.

The Sources of Diversity: Psychological

A second source of human diversity lies in the individual's cognitive, perceptual, and personality development. These psychological structures are closely tied to physiological characteristics through the interplay of genetics and environment. We have seen that human genetics creates potentialities and limits for development. We have also seen that human potential and limits are strongly affected by the socially created environment that facilitates and hinders the development of genetically given potential. Through this process the personality develops. Therefore, "personality is the consequence of the individual's struggle to satisfy his/her drives in the face of social constraints,"[30] and once formed, it establishes distinctive and consistent response patterns to life situations.[31] It is this organized, consistent manner of meeting needs which serves to both distinguish and group people.

The psychological basis for diversity strengthens one's understanding of the importance of the interaction between individuals, groups, and society. As noted earlier, needs exist at both the individual and societal/group levels. Need-meeting behavior at one level must be compatible with that behavior at the other level. Hence, a very creative person must also be able to fit into a whole range of social situations which require some degree of routine and conformity — working at a job, obeying traffic laws, and so on. Yet creative people may also band together to support each other's creative endeavors, recognizing the fact that society may reward conformity more often than creativity. In this way, a group characterized by one type of diversity — here, creativity — results from the joining together of individuals who share this particular psychological characteristic. This example also illustrates that members of a group defined by a difference (creative people) are *similar* with respect to that characteristic (creativity) but also *diverse* with respect to other characteristics. To forget this is to *stereotype** people accord-

---

*Stereotyping is assuming that all members of a group share a range of characteristics or behaviors because they share a particular characteristic, which defines them as a group. For example, women are typically stereotyped as wanting to have children, being overly emotional, liking to gossip, and so on.

ing to the biological, psychological, social, or cultural basis for diversity being used. We will return to this point later in the chapter.

Personality is one of the best-studied bases for diversity, and a host of theories have been offered to explain personality structure and development.[32] Most would agree that "personality is adaptive, learned, influenced by culture, and unique to the individual."[33] Many theorists have concluded that there are *stages* of development in which particular aspects of the environment are especially important for the development of various personality characteristics, such as a sense of trust, autonomy, initiative, and the ability to form loving relationships with others. Theories vary, however, in the importance placed on each stage for the later mastery of succeeding stages. For example, while many Freudian-based theories consider mastery at each stage critical for further development, behavioristic theories see personality as much more flexible and adaptable throughout the life cycle.

Since the relationship of the developing person to the environment is so important for the building of a personality structure capable of balancing individual and social needs, cognitive and perceptual mechanisms are critical. *Perception* is the process by which information is extracted from the environment, making goal-directed behavior possible. Forgus and Shulman state that "Life is an adaptive process and adaptation requires *information*."[34] Coelho and Adams concur, noting that "individual adaptation is a compromise that involves the simultaneous management of three tasks — securing adequate information, maintaining satisfactory internal conditions, and keeping up some degree of autonomy or freedom of action. All of these balancing processes imply learning over time."[35] We can see, then, that people are constantly obtaining and processing information as part of relating to their environments.

A theory of the role of cognitive functions in personality development has been developed by Piaget. This theory shows how the development of cognition progresses from essentially self-centered to highly rational approaches to need-meeting.[36] These changes in the individual's cognitive processing of the environment affect his or her relationships with the environment, especially the sense of mastery and self-control. Cognitive and perceptual components of personality lead back once more to the close link between physiology and psychology. Obviously any type of physiologically based cognitive or perceptual difficulty, such as learning disabilities or deafness, will have implications for personality development. Two implications are especially important: effects on the individual's ability to accurately process information, and the social responses that either accentuate or minimize the effects of the difficulty. A learning disorder can be minimized if it is recognized, accepted, and treated with appropriate therapy. That same disorder may be seriously destructive if it leads to categorizing, stereotyping, and discrimination by society.

Psychology as a basis for human diversity, then, operates at a number of levels. Cognitive and perceptual capacities are closely related to genetic factors that establish individual limits and potential. Cognitive and perceptual development occur through interaction with the social environment that affects the level and type of development. Through the use of cognitive and perceptual mechanisms, information is obtained and processed, leading to personality development. It is personality — an individual's unique patterns of responding to situations — which is the most obvious type of psychologically based diversity. The individual's personality is, of course, affected by physiological characteristics — disabilities, size, sex, age, and so forth — and the social environment that responds to these characteristics. Personality is therefore a composite indicator of an individual and his or her responses to the environment. Again we see how understanding the interaction between all of the sources of human diversity is as important as understanding each by itself.

One last characteristic of personality as a source of human diversity is important. As noted above, the personality is an adaptive structure that helps the individual meet his or her needs within particular social environments. For helping professionals, the emphasis on adaptation is very significant. Personality structures can become rigid and lose their ability to help individuals adapt to their environment. When this happens one usually speaks of a personality disorder. The therapy provided by psychologists and psychiatrists focuses on resolving such disorders, whereas social workers focus on ways the environment can reduce destructive stresses and help support adaptive efforts by individuals. For social workers and related helping professionals, understanding the psychological bases for human diversity should emphasize ways in which people and environments interact so as to respect personality differences and find more effective strategies for mutual support.

The Bases for Diversity: Social-Structural

The process of *differentiating* between people has characterized every known society, although the criteria used for this purpose have varied considerably.[37] Age and sex are universal differentiating criteria; also common are race, ethnicity (including tribal identity), religion, socioeconomic standing, physical characteristics, and sexual orientation. The effects of differentiation are also wideranging.[38] Some societies differentiate in order to allocate tasks. In these cases, the criteria of differentiation are assumed to relate to the individual's ability to perform tasks assigned to him or her. For example, elderly people may be assigned child care responsibilities rather than labor in the fields, or members of one racial group may be assigned menial work because a society deems it appropriate to their presumed genetic limitations. The accuracy of the relationship between differentiating criteria and assigned tasks is less important than the social reality created by the system of differentiation. As Mechanic has paraphrased, "if men define situations as real, they are real in their consequences."[39]

Differentiating between people need not lead to stratification, although it frequently does. *Social stratification* is a system of differentiation that leads to the hierarchal ranking of people from high to low, upper to lower, and so forth.[40] For example, India has a rigid caste system that clearly ranks people from high to low castes. One's caste determines most of an individual's life experiences from health care to education to employment to chances of living and dying. Sometimes differentiation shades into stratification, as is illustrated by the case of women in the United States. While sex is ostensibly only a differentiating criterion, in fact it is a stratifying criterion that leads to women's being treated as inferior to men.[41] For example, women are assigned child care responsibilities because of a presumed "maternal instinct." This unproven "instinct" has the effect of keeping women either out of the labor force or in restricted careers due to their working part time or dropping in and out of the work force in order to perform their assigned child-bearing and child-rearing roles. The reduced economic opportunities which result then make women economically dependent on men, who perform the societally assigned "breadwinner" role. This economic dependence has obvious implications for women's power vis-a-vis men and their ability to participate in the institutions of society.

Society, then, clearly differentiates between groups of people. The diverse groups that result are then assigned different tasks and functions in society which in turn affect the life chances and life styles of the members of these various groups. Before discussing how people become members of these groups, we must summarize two sociological concepts: position and role. *Position* refers to a group of people who share both a title and characteristic behaviors.[42] For example, "homosexual" is a position in that homosexual people share this title and have intimate relationships with others of the same sex. The behavior shared by members of a position is their *role*. A nurse (position) is expected to care for patients, keep medical charts accurately, confer with doctors, and so forth — these behaviors make up the nurse's role. Similarly, the role of social workers is to interview clients, keep accurate records of client contacts, join the professional association, advocate for client needs with agency directors, and so forth.

People are placed in positions (and therefore roles) in two ways.[43] Positions may be *achieved*, meaning they may be chosen. Social worker, wife, ballet dancer, bridge player, automobile driver, and home owner are all examples of achieved positions. Other positions are *ascribed*, or allocated to people whether or not they want them. Son, cancer victim, woman, infant, and Caucasian are all ascribed positions. Some positions have elements of both achievement and ascription. These include ethnicity (we are born into an ethnic group but can deny or change our ethnic identity) and, similarly, religion. Obviously we all occupy many, many positions at the same time. Some of our positions come to us because of our biological characteristics, which constitute one type of ascription. We are born male or female, for example. While we may be in a position for biological reasons, the impact of membership on our life style and life chances is socially determined. Once again the close relationship between biological and social sources of behavior is illustrated.

Positions and their associated roles establish societal expectations for people. In this way, positions help give direction to people's lives — social workers know how to go about their work, housewives know how to organize their days, and so on. However, in most cases positions and roles reflect the values of dominant groups in society and may serve to perpetuate discrimination against other groups. This occurs in two principal ways. One is that roles *teach* certain people that they are unimportant — Blacks and Native Americans often learn this, as do many women, old people, and people with physical disabilities.[44] The second is by having roles defined in such a way as to cause others to *expect* undesirable behavior (as defined by dominant groups) from members of denigrated groups — women are expected to be hysterical, Blacks to be lazy, Native Americans drunk, old people forgetful, and physically disabled people helpless. These expectations tend to influence how people act toward members of such minority groups, as well as others' interpretation of behaviors by members of these groups.[45] For example, many Blacks use the English language differently from the dominant group. This is taken as evidence of their ignorance rather than as an indicator of cultural difference in spite of research demonstrating that their use of English has its own grammatical structure and logic.

In addition to affecting expectations of others, positions and roles affect the expectations of group members themselves. Doctors learn to think of themselves as important while many women learn to think of their work as relatively unimportant. People without physical disabilities define and organize the world around themselves; the disabled learn that they have to struggle in a difficult and often hostile world which ignores their needs. Young adults view the future with optimism; the elderly frequently have their boundaries narrowed and come to feel useless and hopeless. Through the process of assigning people to positions (and roles), society creates kinds of differences that affect the basic fabric of people's lives. Depending on the group to which one belongs, one will be treated well or badly by dominant groups, will be provided or denied opportunities, and will have a sense of well-being or of fear, anger, and resentment. Here it is again important to note that the criteria used to define positions are societally selected, and the way positions are stratified is also a societal process. Therefore, the structure of society is itself an extremely important source of human diversity.

Roles, by defining behavior expected of occupants of a position, reflect societal norms. *Norms* are societally defined rules for behavior, telling us how we are supposed to act.[46] Therefore, they reflect society's values — what the dominant groups in society consider good and bad, desirable and undesirable, acceptable and unacceptable. Norms can help one develop a positive sense of self by promoting behaviors that society rewards and considers useful. As a social worker, for example, one not only learns what to do in practice but that such behaviors are helpful for society as a whole. Some groups, however, learn that what they do — indeed, what they are expected to do — is not worthwhile, or only minimally so. For example, an unmarried mother receiving public assistance quickly learns that her efforts to raise her children are considered inadequate no matter how hard she tries. It comes as no surprise, then, that such behavior is poorly rewarded, thereby making it more difficult for members of such groups to develop a positive sense of self.

Obviously, then, the concept of *normative behavior*, or behavior that reflects social norms, has two aspects. On one hand, norms are used to describe expected behavior resulting from societal definitions of what is desirable. These expectations reflect the values of dominant groups. On the other hand, norms are used to judge behavior. That which is different from the norm is not only different, it is also less good. As Grinker notes, "Concepts of 'health' and 'normality' have sometimes been used as the common ground for interdisciplinary discussions, but these terms have increasingly been seen as heavily charged with value judgments and as actually representing often fictional states."[47] If societies were uniform so that decisions in fact represented a consensus, norms would be objective descriptions of the desirable. However, in a highly diverse society, what is desirable and useful for one group is often undesirable and hurtful to others. Indeed, those groups with the most power attempt to define normative behavior as what they themselves do and that thus maintains the status quo, which benefits them. Therefore, social workers must approach concepts of normality and health with care so that they don't become blinded to the ways they may be used to disadvantage diverse groups. For example, deafness is non-normative, and the deaf are routinely excluded from principal information channels as a result. But should communication be controlled by hearing persons or should it be something society routinely makes available to everyone in whatever forms are necessary?

Deviance is behavior which violates a norm. It is the reverse of normativeness, and it too may be used to judge behavior rather than simply describe it. Deviance is used by dominant groups as a label for behavior that needs to be controlled.[48] Here again definitions of what is acceptable and what needs to be controlled primarily reflect social power. Some behavior defined as deviant by dominant groups is useful for the groups who perform it. The reason for its being defined as unacceptable is that it may threaten the advantaged position of the dominant group. In these situations, privileged groups often have enough power to use the deviance label as justification for trying to control the behavior. For example, paying mothers who are poor to stay at home to care for their young children seems a perfectly reasonable strategy for child-rearing. Indeed, society generally expects women to perform this task. However, poor mothers are pushed into the labor market as soon as possible even though the quality of care their children receive suffers, and even though society may have to pay for alternative child care facilities, such as day care. This occurs because poor women represent a source of cheap labor valuable to persons who control decision making and economic power. The label of deviance is used in two ways. Laws exist that force poor mothers to work, except under certain specified conditions. Therefore if they do not work, they are legally deviant — they have broken the law. In addition, a *stigma** is attached to receipt of financial aid. Any woman who receives it suffers the loss of a personal sense of worth — a nonlegal consequence of deviance.

---

*A stigma is the social devaluation of a person because of a socially undesirable characteristic, such as a physical disfigurement, or because of having performed a socially unacceptable behavior.

Obviously the only way out of these complications is to return to the dual perspective. While a set of generalized societal values usually prevail, different groups interpret and elaborate on these values in multiple ways. Ethnic and racial groups modify societal norms, sometimes considerably, as can be seen in different groups' attitudes toward size of families, importance of extended family structures, abortion, financial success, language patterns, child-rearing patterns, and others.[49] All groups confront societal norms according to the way they impinge on the behavior of the group's members. Nevertheless the norms governing behavior within diverse groups may not be accepted outside the group. From the point of view of the dominant society, such behaviors may be considered deviant and therefore unacceptable. For this reason, members of diverse groups often lead two lives — one within the boundaries of the diverse group itself, following its norms, and the other in situations where the norms of the dominant society are enforced.

Reconciling the two different perspectives is essentially the process of social change, which is constantly going on. Yet as long as definitions of deviance are imposed on diverse groups, their members are subject to *negative sanctions** which seek to bring their behavior into conformity with dominant societal norms. Denigrating group behavior, teaching group members negative self-images, and rewarding societally normative behavior are all strategies to change the behavior of members of diverse groups. Stereotyping is often used to exaggerate behavior defined by the dominant society as deviant. For example, the elderly are characterized by dominant groups in our society as slow, forgetful, and living in the past — all attributes devalued by our society's current focus on youthfulness. This pressures old people to act and look younger than they are and to keep out of many activities such as work, sports, many types of entertainment, and so on.[†]

---

*A sanction is a socially defined response to a behavior. A positive sanction rewards behavior, whereas a negative sanction indicates social disapproval.

†It should be noted that a number of minority groups value the elderly. This is true among most Hispanic and Native American cultures, for example.

Discriminatory behavior is built into the social structure through social institutions.

> The generalizing of dominant group power promotes patterns of *institutionalized discrimination*, which means *systematic discrimination through the regular operation of societal institutions.* All the members of dominant groups, including those who personally do not discriminate and who do not favor the system, receive the benefits of institutionalized discrimination against minorities.[50]

Institutionalized discrimination, in practice, means that minority group members earn less for the same work and generally have less desirable jobs, worse housing, less education, a higher incidence of poverty and unemployment, poorer health, shorter life spans, and a host of other disadvantageous life characteristics.[51] Perhaps the most succinct summary of the impact on people's lives of being a minority group member is given by Saenz:

> Within the culture of this country an individual is perceived as mentally healthy when he or she is capable of adapting to his or her life conditions, when he or she has the ability to resolve problems by assuming the values of the dominant society. But when an individual's adaptation differs from the values of the majority, that person is seen as deviant, mentally disturbed, delinquent, or criminal and, more often than not, is punished, not treated.[52]

All in all, society's attempts to control those it has defined as deviant can be extremely powerful. While behavior that threatens human life or well-being should be controlled, efforts to control behavior that results from biological or cultural diversity often spring from a desire to protect power and advantage rather than human life or well-being.

To conclude, the social structure is a powerful creator of diversity because it differentiates between groups of people. The criteria used to differentiate usually include biological and psychological characteristics as well as other criteria created by societies themselves. Social structures also modify biological sources of diversity to incorporate them into social-structural sources of diversity. To illustrate, race is a biological source of diversity but societies define whether race will be a basis for stratifying and/or differentiating. The subsequent effects on people's lives are obviously quite different if race is used only to differentiate or also to stratify. Social structure as a basis for diversity grows out of societal values and leads to the assignment of people to groups. Once assigned, group members experience predictable life chances and life styles that essentially determine the quality of their lives.

Social structure is the most immediately significant source of diversity in people's lives. Since social definitions can override biological or psychological realities, societal expectations are critical determinants of what happens to people. For example, although Jews are an ethnic/religious group rather than a race, the fact that they were defined as a race in Nazi Germany, where racism was particularly rampant, led to their persecution. Once people are socially defined as a group, their identity develops around that definition. A distinctive diverse group is the result, a group whose sense of identity and behavior patterns differentiate it from other groups. Ironically, though a group's sense of identity may result from societal definitions, once it exists it may provide the basis for changing the societal definition. So, for example, persecution led to Blacks developing a collective identity that has been used to shape society's efforts toward greater understanding and fairer treatment of Blacks.[53] Once more, employing the dual perspective is essential. A group defined as deviant by the dominant society experiences social institutions in disadvantageous ways. While in few groups is most behavior defined as deviant, in many, particular aspects of behavior or identity are so defined. Whereas women, for example, are not generally considered deviant, a woman's sexually aggressive behavior may be. Understanding these variations — many of which are rather subtle — is important for understanding particular responses to situations. Because the power of social structures to define and organize behavior is so great, one part of professional helping efforts must always include activities to change societal definitions that arbitrarily disadvantage members of diverse groups.

The Bases of Diversity: Cultural

Culture is learned, shared, and transmitted behavior.[54] Societies are structures that organize the day-to-day behavior needed to operationalize a culture. Put another way, culture is the storehouse of values, knowledge, behaviors, and objects that are available to a group of people. However, not all groups have what could be considered a culture. Culture characterizes groups that are enduring and that pass on information and traditions from one generation to another. Such groups include ethnic and racial groups, religious groups, nationality groups, occupational groups, gender groups (little girls learn to act like their mothers, for example), and sexual preference groups (homosexuals are taught the knowledge and traditions of their group when they "come out" and are socialized into the subculture).[55] Other groups have somewhat weaker cultures. Age groups vary in the degree to which they pass on knowledge and traditions, as do physical disability and socioeconomic groups. The growth of a clear sense of group identity usually facilitates the development of a culture. The more the disabled and the elderly recognize and accept their group membership, for example, the more likely it will be that values, knowledge, behaviors, and objects distinctive to these groups will be preserved and transmitted over time.

Clearly culture is a complex phenomenon. To illustrate, a nationality-based culture characterizes the United States as a whole. Within this nation, however, there are many, many subgroups that have their own variations on the larger culture. These subgroups are often called *subcultures*, and include the range of racial, ethnic, religious, and other groups noted above, each of which has its own culture.[56] This multiplicity of subcultures within a larger culture is characteristic of large, complex industrialized societies. Another way to look at the relationship between the whole and its parts is to speak in terms of a *dominant culture* (the whole) and *minority cultures* (the parts). Davis notes that "groups differ in *power*, which means *the ability to determine the outcomes of group interaction*. The concept of minority-dominant relations implies group differences in power, since dominant groups are able to subject minorities to unequal treatment."[57]

As we discussed in the previous section, definitions developed by the dominant culture affect the minority cultures. For example, if Poles are defined as dim-witted by the majority culture there will be derogatory "Polish jokes" regardless of how rich Polish-American culture may be or how intelligent most Polish people are.

All people have to manage relationships between the dominant culture and minority cultures. Their minority cultures, transmitted and maintained through group memberships discussed in the previous section, are important parts of themselves — how they think, what they value, how they act. These have to be incorporated into the expectations of the dominant culture. Usually minority cultures have worked out procedures for relating to other cultures. Puerto Ricans on the United States mainland, for example, often clearly segmentalize the contexts in which they operationalize their membership in a subculture, such as at home, and those in which they act like members of the dominant culture, such as at work or at school. Even so, problems may develop. This is especially likely when minority cultures feel that the dominant culture seeks to denigrate or even destroy their cultures, a phenomenon called *cultural imperialism*. Fortunately, in the United States there is increasing emphasis on *cultural pluralism*, whereby the integrity and value of subcultures is recognized and respected by the dominant culture.[58] It is certainly the case that the acceptance of cultural pluralism makes it easier for people to manage the diversity that results from their multiple cultural memberships.

Professional Purpose and Human Diversity

Goldschmidt notes that we must conscientiously seek ways of establishing institutionalized means for individuals to cope with an ever-changing society in order that they may preserve an adequate sense of self."[59] Mechanic continues that idea, stating, "Man's abilities to cope with the environment depend on the efficacy of the solutions that his culture provides, and the skills he develops are dependent on the adequacy of the preparatory institutions to which he has been exposed."[60] The issue is clear: people depend on social structure for their own survival and happiness, and the social structure can itself only endure if people's needs are met appropriately. Social work's commitment is to improving the nature of this exchange between people and their environments, and the idea of human diversity is a powerful tool in helping the profession operationalize this commitment.

While all four sources of diversity are important for understanding human behavior, social structure is the most important for understanding how the social environment facilitates or inhibits people's sense of self and the adequacy with which they are able to cope with the environment. Dominant groups benefit most from societal arrangements, and it is obviously in their best interest to preserve the status quo. In order for this to happen, minority groups must continue to be excluded from political (decision-making) or economic (resource) power. How is this to occur when, in a democratic society, everyone is supposed to have equal access to the political and economic institutions?

The task is accomplished in two principal ways. The first is an inevitable result of the existing stratification of groups in society. While access to power and resources may be open to all, people begin the race to obtain them from very different places. This ensures that for the most part those who already have a privileged position will maintain it. To help them even further, a second strategy is employed — stereotyping. In this strategy, ideologies are created to justify existing inequities based on the highly selective use and misuse of information about members of diverse groups. In combination, these two strategies create a self-perpetuating system in which minority groups are disadvantaged and their disadvantage is justified on the basis of stereotypes and ideologies. These stereotypes function to maintain the privilege of those groups that create and use them. Naturally they are dysfunctional for the groups they are used against.

Currently the dominant group in United States society is highly educated Caucasian males. This group controls the nation's major corporations and elected and appointed governmental positions, thus ensuring control over the most important decision-making and economic structures. Starting from this reality, it is not difficult to see how stereotypes are created and used to justify the exclusion of as many groups as possible from this elite group. Let's look at some of them. Non-Caucasians and non-males are easily dealt with. Blacks are portrayed as lazy and ignorant, Orientals as cunning and untrustworthy, Native Americans as drunkards, and women as emotional and uninterested in matters of business and politics. Through the careful nurturance of such stereotypes institutionalized systems of discrimination channel members of these groups outside the loci of decision-making and economic power.

It is even more revealing to look at how stereotypes are created to exclude from the elite groups of potentially eligible Caucasian males. Age proves to be a useful device. The young are said to be too "hot-headed" and untrained, allowing time to make sure they are co-opted into, rather than challenging, the existing structure. Considering the elderly too frail and disoriented provides an effective mechanism for upward mobility within the elite. Treating ethnicity as if it were race excludes Hispanics and a whole range of other groups that are not seen as "Caucasian." The handicapped are defined as incapable of handling the demands of jobs, whether or not that is in fact true in individual cases. Finally, homosexuals are considered too dangerous since they, and hence those with whom they interact, could face public embarrassment if they were to be arrested. Besides, since homosexuals are stereotyped as effeminate, they are defined as not altogether male and are therefore ineligible.

In such a system of interlocking stereotypes and discrimination, it is little wonder people try desperately to appear acceptable. Ethnic people change their names; people falsify their ages and use a variety of means to appear younger; women adopt appropriate "executive" dress such as suits and short hair styles; homosexuals go to extraordinary lengths to hide their affectional preference, including entering into marriages of convenience. Here is where the social worker must use the concept of human diversity to disentangle the convoluted means these various groups use to meet their needs through the existing social structure. Given the substantial price minority groups pay in terms of life chances and life styles, it is little wonder people want to evade the stereotypes that are used to condemn them to minority status. Yet the costs in terms of loss of identity, personal fear, and self-denigration are often also very great.

People *are* different because of biological, psychological, and cultural factors. But social structures should support the translation of these differences into satisfying lives rather than defining them as undesirable traps to be avoided. Ganter and Yeakel express the social work perspective when they say, "Respect for differences implies social support for the integrity of all groups of society, and increases the opportunity to learn from the variety of human experiences that differences represent."[61] A social work practitioner who cannot use the idea of human diversity to understand how people are different and what their needs are as a result of their particular characteristics cannot help people live more satisfying lives. However, the ways in which the social structure operates to support and respect human differences is an essential context within which to help people find the resources they need. This perspective will help identify those parts of the social structure that need to be modified in order to better distribute opportunities and resources to *all* people in a society.

Summary

Human diversity is a simple fact of life. Our biological make-up, our psychological functioning, our social-structural environment,

FIGURE 3.2

Human Diversity's Influences on Behavior

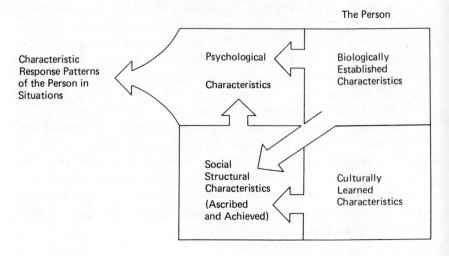

and our cultural memberships all serve to express differences between people. Figure 3.2 summarizes the ways diversity is expressed in human behavior.

Understanding these relationships necessitates mastery of basic concepts from the social, biological, and behavioral sciences. The perspective of human diversity in turn provides a focus for the integration of concepts from these several sciences. As the diagram above illustrates, for example, cultural factors influence social structures, which in turn affect the way people perceive and organize the world around them. It is evident that the systems and human diversity perspectives together help to explain human behavior. The following chapter will show how human diversity is also helpful for understanding that different groups use different methods to meet the same needs — in other words, that people's behavior is goal-directed even though we may have difficulty understanding its purposes because they differ from our own.

Study Questions

1. Look at yourself from the perspective of human diversity. In what ways are you different from others you know? Rank the differences in terms of those that have the most influence on your life and those that have the least. Then examine the difference that you have selected as the most significant in your life. Identify as many areas of your life as you can that are affected by this difference. Has it ever been a source of problems? Is help available to deal with those problems? What kind of help? Did you ever use it? Why or why not?

2. The chapter cautions that social workers have to understand diversity *between* groups as well as within one group. Select an ethnic group about which you are knowledgeable. Use at least five other types of diversity (socioeconomic, age, religion, and so forth) to analyze the diversity within the ethnic group you have selected. Does such an analysis help you to understand the group better? Why or why not?

3. All of us have strong feelings about certain diverse groups. Some find it difficult to accept the physically handicapped, for example, while others don't like to be around the elderly. Which diverse groups do you have difficulty *accepting* even though *intellectually* you may understand them? Examine your feelings about these groups carefully. What do you think is the basis of your feelings? How do the feelings affect your behavior? Do you think you could modify your feelings and behavior so that you could do professional social work with members of the group in question? Do you feel an obligation to engage in these modifications? If not, how would you deal with a client from the group in question?

4. Select a group that would be considered a diverse group according to the criteria discussed in this chapter (women, homosexuals, the physically limited, and so on). Analyze the group and decide whether it has a culture. Justify your decision. Then examine the particular resources and obstacles members of this group have. In your opinion, are the resources or the obstacles more significant in their efforts to live satisfying lives? Here again, be sure to support your opinion.

5. Find a newspaper article that illustrates either the *use of* or *need for* the dual perspective. Explain in detail which is illustrated and how. Then examine how the use or non-use of the dual perspective has influenced the content and conclusions in the article. Finally, briefly discuss the importance of the dual perspective for social workers, using your newspaper article analysis as an example.

Notes

1. For an excellent discussion and elaboration of this point within the context of the provision of health care services, see Ann Templeton Brownlee, *Community, Culture, and Care* (St. Louis: C. V. Mosby, 1978).

2. Anna S. Ochoa and Susan K. Schuster, "Social Studies Instruction for Handicapped Children," in *The Link* 3, no. 5 (May 1980), p. 2.

3. Dolores G. Norton, *The Dual Perspective* (New York: Council on Social Work Education, 1978), pp. 3–12.

4. Betty Berzon and Robert Leighton, eds., *Positively Gay* (Millbrae, Ca.: Celestial Arts, 1979), pp. 1–14, 30–50, 78, 87–100, 109–111, 145, 182–187.

5. Allan Bell and Martin Weinberg, *Homosexualities* (New York: Simon and Schuster, 1978).

6. E. Carrington Boggan, Marilyn G. Faft, Charles Lister, and John P. Rupp, *The Rights of Gay People* (New York: Avon Books, 1975). The National Gay Task Force, 80 Fifth Ave., New York, N.Y., has a range of informational publications including "Twenty Questions About Homosexuality."

7. Walter Goldschmidt, "Ethology, Ecology, and Ethnological Relations," in George V. Coelho, David Hamburg, and John E. Adams, eds., *Coping and Adaptation* (New York: Basic Books, 1974), p. 411.

8. Abraham Maslow, *Motivation and Personality*, 2nd ed. (New York: Harper & Row, 1970), pp. 35–46.

9. Ronald Forgus and Bernard Schulman, *Personality: A Cognitive View* (Englewood Cliffs, N.J.: Prentice-Hall, 1979), p. 121.

10. Ibid., p. 62.

11. Charlotte Towle, *Common Human Needs*, rev. ed. (New York: National Association of Social Workers, 1965), pp. 6–11.

12. Stan Steiner, *The Island* (New York: Harper & Row, 1974), pp. 147–163.

13. Maslow, p. 38.

14. Forgus and Shulman, pp. 30–58.

15. Margot Hornblower, "Hmongtana: Laotian Tribe Starts Over in Bewildering New World," *Washington Post*, 5 July, 1980, pp. A-1, A-6.

16. Allan Mazur and Leon Robertson, p. 39.

17. Ibid.

18. Jane H. Underwood, *Human Variation and Human Micro-Evolution* (Englewood Cliffs, N.J.: Prentice-Hall, 1979), p. 21.

19. Richard Goldsby, *Race and Races* (New York: Macmillan, 1971).

20. Jews, for example, are particularly susceptible to Tay-Sachs disease. Other ethnic groups have similar susceptibilities to other diseases. See Underwood, pp. 20–38.

21. Goldsby, pp. 5–13.

22. F. James Davis, *Minority-Dominant Relations* (Arlington Heights, Ill.: AHM Publishing, 1978), pp. 88–97.

23.   Howard Bahr, Bruce Chadwick, and Joseph Strauss, *American Ethnicity* (Lexington, Mass.: D.C. Heath, 1979), pp. 290–339, 405–431.

24.   Mazur and Robertson, p. 91.

25.   Ibid., pp. 52–53.

26.   Ibid., p. 35.

27.   Alison Clarke-Stewart, *Child Care in the Family* (New York: Academic Press, 1977), pp. 11–63.

28.   Underwood, p. 30.

29.   Harold M. Schmeck, Jr., "Advances in Gene-splicing Spur Debate on Regulating Production," *New York Times*, 9 June 1980, pp. A-1, A-7.

30.   Forgus and Shulman, p. 22.

31.   Ibid., p. 2.

32.   There are any number of relatively concise anthologies of personality theories. Two that can be recommended are Jonas Langer, *Theories of Development* (New York: Holt, Rinehart, and Winston, 1969), and Alfred Baldwin, *Theories of Child Development* (New York: John Wiley, 1968).

33.   Forgus and Shulman, p. 2.

34.   Ibid., p. 136.

35.   George Coelho and John Adams, "Introduction," in Coelho, Hamburg, Adams, p. XIX.

36.   Barry Wadsworth, *Piaget's Theory of Cognitive Development*, 2nd ed. (N.Y.: Longman, 1979).

37.   Ronald C. Federico, *Sociology*, 2nd ed. (Reading, Mass.: Addison-Wesley, 1979), pp. 149–167.

38.   Lucile Duberman, *Social Inequality* (Philadelphia: J.B. Lippincott, 1976), pp. 1–21.

39.   David Mechanic, "Social Structure and Personal Adaptation: Some Neglected Dimensions," in Coelho, Hamburg, Adams, p. 38.

40.   Federico, pp. 149–167.

41.   Elizabeth McTaggart Almquist, *Minorities, Gender, and Work* (Lexington, Mass.: Lexington Books, 1979).

42.   Federico, pp. 95–111. See also Grace Ganter and Margaret Yeakel, *Human Behavior and the Social Environment* (New York: Columbia University Press, 1980), pp. 96–105.

43.   Federico, pp. 98–108.

44. Bahr, Chadwick, Strauss, pp. 284–313.

45. Davis, pp. 43–63.

46. Federico, pp. 41–47.

47. Roy R. Grinker Sr., "Foreword," in Coelho, Hamburg, Adams, p. XI.

48. See also Ganter and Yeakel, pp. 107–113.

49. Bahr, Chadwick, Strauss. See also Almquist.

50. Davis, p. 30.

51. See Bahr, Chadwick, Strauss; Davis; and Almquist for more extensive discussion of these points, as well as voluminous supporting data.

52. Javier Saenz, "The Value of a Humanistic Model in Serving Hispanic Families," in Miguel Monteil, ed., *Hispanic Families* (Washington, D.C.: National Coalition of Hispanic Mental Health and Human Service Organizations, 1978), p. 11.

53. Bahr, Chadwick, Strauss, pp. 328–336, 524–547.

54. Federico, pp. 31–34.

55. Frances Hanckel and John Cunningham, *A Way of Love, A Way of Life* (New York: Lothrop, Lee and Shepard Books, 1979).

56. Davis, p. 5.

57. Ibid., p. 29.

58. Ibid., pp. 151–163, 285–292.

59. Goldschmidt, p. 29.

60. Mechanic, p. 33.

61. Ganter and Yeakel, p. 289.

Additional Readings

Bahr, Howard; Chadwick, Bruce; and Day, Robert. *Native Americans Today: Sociological Perspectives.* New York: Harper & Row, 1972.

Billingsley, Andrew and Giovanni, Jeanne M. *Children of the Storm: Black Children and American Child Welfare.* New York: Harcourt Brace Jovanovich, 1972.

Boston Women's Health Collective. *Our Bodies, Our Selves.* Rev. ed. New York: Simon and Schuster, 1976.

Bowe, Frank. *Handicapping America: Barriers to Disabled People.* New York: Harper & Row, 1978.

Cordasco, Francesco, and Bucchioni, Eugene. *The Puerto Rican Experience.* Totowa, N.J.: Littlefield Adams, 1973.

Cottle, Thomas J. *Black Children, White Dreams.* Boston: Houghton Mifflin, 1974.

Cowan, Paul. *The Tribes of America.* Garden City, N.Y.: Doubleday and Company, 1979.

Feagin, Joe R. and Feagin, Clairece Booker. *Discrimination American Style: Institutional Racism and Sexism.* Englewood Cliffs, N.J.: Prentice-Hall, 1978.

Gochros, Harvey L., and Gochros, Jean S., eds. *The Sexually Oppressed.* New York: Association Press, 1977.

Goodman, James A., ed. *Dynamics of Racism in Social Work Practice.* Washington D.C.: National Association of Social Workers, 1973.

Jenkins, Shirley. *The Ethnic Dilemma in Social Services.* Riverside, N.J.: The Free Press, 1981.

Katz, Jonathan. *Gay American History: Lesbians and Gay Men in the U.S.A.* New York: Avon Books, 1976.

Kephart, William M. *Extraordinary Groups: The Sociology of Unconventional Life Styles.* New York: St. Martin's Press, 1976.

Ladner, Joyce T. *Tomorrow's Tomorrow: The Black Woman.* Garden City, N.Y.: Anchor Books, 1971.

Long, Elton; Long, James; Leon, Wilma; and Weston, Paul B. *American Minorities: The Justice Issue.* Englewood Cliffs, N.J.: Prentice-Hall, 1975.

Norman, Elaine, and Mancuso, Arlene. *Women's Issues and Social Work Practice.* Itasca, Ill.: F. E. Peacock, 1980.

Sidel, Ruth. *Urban Survival: The World of Working-Class Women.* Boston: Beacon Press, 1978.

Snyder, Eloise C., ed. *The Study of Women: Enlarging Perspectives of Social Reality.* New York: Harper & Row, 1979.

Tyler, Gus, ed. *Mexican-Americans Tomorrow: Educational and Economic Prospects.* Albuquerque, N.M.: University of New Mexico Press, 1975.

U.S. Commission on Civil Rights. *Puerto Ricans in the Continental United States: An Uncertain Future.* Washington, D.C.: U.S. Commission on Civil Rights, 1976.

We encounter here an
important principle in human
behavior: No matter how
unusual an individual's
behavior may seem to us it has
its rational foundation, its logic.
His behavior, like ours, is
serving him some useful
purpose in the maintenance of
a kind of equilibrium, that is, a
state of comfort in his life.

Charlotte Towle[1]

CHAPTER 4

Goal-Directed Behavior

Introduction

This chapter will extend the systems and human diversity perspectives discussed in the previous two chapters and look specifically at how human behavior is focused on the attainment of life goals. Starting with the assumption that human behavior is not random, the interrelated ideas of need satisfaction, drives, purpose, adaptation, and coping will be discussed. Examples from practice will be used as illustrations. This chapter will further discuss how different strategies are employed by different groups to attain life goals. It will emphasize how each strategy is used in uniquely purposeful goal-directed ways. Understanding human behavior from the perspective of goal direction and purpose is essential for developing professional helping strategies that involve people in the helping process and that build on their strengths.

The simultaneous focus on person and environment that characterizes the profession of social work calls for an understanding of the forces that generate and guide the behavior of both individuals and larger social aggregates. For example, in order for a practitioner in a public assistance agency to design effective intervention strategies that take into account the reciprocal influences of persons and environments, it is essential that he or she understand the forces directing the behavior of the client population, the welfare bureaucracy, and the larger publics that support or defeat social legislation. Were all these component parts of the public assistance system to share a common sense of purpose and direction, the task of intervention would indeed be a far simpler one. This, however, is often not the case. The recipient, the social worker, the administrator, and the politically motivated adversary usually perceive the welfare system differently. The individual and institutional goals based on these perceptions may therefore be incompatible, if not in direct conflict. So, for example, advocating for the rights of the recipient is consistent with the goals of the social work profession. However, doing so may put the social worker in jeopardy with his or her employing organization, one of whose goals may be to stop the growth of the welfare rolls.

The extreme variability evidenced in human behavior makes it impossible to come to any common definition of purpose, or goal direction, as a motivation of human behavior. The reality of the person-situation configuration attests to the fact that people are always managing many purposes at once. It is through social systems, and the non-human systems that impinge on their behavior, that these multiple purposes are meshed. As a guideline or motivating force for action, purpose demands of the behaving unit the ability to juggle multiple and often conflicting purposes simultaneously. The course of action (goal-directed behavior) that is planned should assure a comfortable fit with the environment.

Motivation, Needs, and Purpose

Motivation as a force directing behavior has captured the imagination of philosopher and social scientist alike. The ancient Greeks believed behavior was determined by the relationship between body fluids, which they called humors, and the different temperaments — sanguine, melancholic, and phlegmatic.[2] This served as an explanation for purposeful behavior. Bergson's idea of "élan vital" and William James' "springs of action" are also examples of attributing goal-directed behavior to factors inherent in the individual's constitutional make-up. Theories abound, frequently reflecting the bias of the discipline purporting them. The nature/nurture argument is a case in point. Motivation has been variously attributed to inheritance (biological factors, or "nature"), to learning (social processes, or "nurture"), and to the interaction of the two. In spite of the different views as to its sources, it is generally agreed that *motivation* refers to the factors stimulating behavior or, in James' colorful phrase, the "springs of action". There are a number of types of motivation, some of which are general and some of which are activated only in specific situations. For clarity of presentation, these factors will be discussed in the context of needs.

Understanding motivation, then, develops from understanding needs. As we have already seen, needs are both biological and social. As a biological system the human organism has certain needs that must be met if it is to survive. While it is commonly known that food and water are basic to human life, it is less well understood how particular types of nutrients — protein, carbohydrates, vitamins, minerals, and so on — are needed for the various parts of the system to interact in a healthy way. This, of course, automatically brings us to social needs, in the form of the question, "What is healthy?" Biologists might answer this question in terms of what is minimally necessary for organic survival and development. Others, however, might have very different goals in mind. Is healthy a state of one's own perception — feeling well? Is it a state of appearance — fitting a social model of physical attractiveness? Or is it perhaps the ability to work for a certain period of time without tiring — the typical eight-hour work day in United States society? The point is biological needs are interpreted by people and become expressed in social terms.[3] An understanding of human diversity allows us to predict that different groups will interpret biological needs somewhat differently. For example, in orthodox Jewish culture questions of nutrition are filtered through the cultural values encoded in kosher dietary laws.

In addition to the cultural elaboration of biological needs, culture creates purely social needs. Let us take as an example the production and distribution of resources. When societies decide to *industrialize*, or to substitute mechanical power for human and animal power, they commit themselves to a sequence of social processes which affects all aspects of the social structure. Industrialization has a number of social-structural effects: urbanization, a decrease in the number of people involved in agriculture, a shift toward the nuclear family, more centralized government, a money economy, and a rise in the general standard of living. These processes impact differently on various segments of a society, but all gradually share an emerging social need — the need to industrialize. As a result, people move to cities, seek jobs in order to get money, and aspire to the material goods that industrialization makes possible — cars, fashionable clothes, indoor plumbing, books, and the like. These aspirations become perceived as needs as powerful as biological needs. This is because humans, because of their genetically endowed flexibility, have to survive in a highly structured social world as well as in a physical world.

Both physical and social needs function as *drives*, or powerful motivators for behavior.[4] Motivation for actions, then, comes from the drive to do something in order to meet a perceived need which may be biological, social, or, most commonly, some combination of both. Needs become *internalized*, that is, part of the person's basic sense of self.[5] However, what exactly gets internalized as a need varies according to people's diverse group memberships. The social elaboration of biological needs, as well as the creation and interpretation of social needs, varies from group to group. Puerto Rico provides an interesting example. Puerto Rico is part of the United States, yet is separated from the mainland, is an island, and enjoys a tropical climate. In addition, historically it is closely tied to Indian and Spanish cultures. As a result, the typical Puerto Rican diet consists of common United States products liberally mixed with fresh fruits. The effects of industrialization are modified by a still strong extended family structure, less concern with punctuality, and a belief that interpersonal relationships are at least as important as purely commercial relationships. Need-meeting for many Puerto Ricans, therefore, is perceived somewhat differently than for mainland residents of the United States even though the ultimate biological and social needs are similar. This is a type of *selective perception** that results from diverse group memberships and affects the way in which needs function as drives.[6] Everyone has needs, and for everyone these needs function as drives. What the needs are must be understood in part in the context of the biological characteristics of the human species, but more importantly within the context of human diversity.

Needs and goals are combined and organized so that motivation for action is focused around *goals* and a sense of *purpose*. Purposive action means behavior directed toward some goal, a desired event. The attainment of the goal "is said to be the purpose of one's action or striving."[7] Observation of the behavior of nonhuman primates indicates that it is guided primarily by physiological, that is biological, needs:

---

*Selective perception refers to the fact that people observe most closely that part of their environment which is of particular importance or interest to them. This can, of course, lead to rather inaccurate and incomplete observations.

... nutritional, reproductive, life preservation, pain avoiding. Actually these needs overlap; the need to avoid freezing to death can pretty much modify an animal's need to reproduce. The animal seems driven to do certain things beyond the gratification of a need. In other words the motivation seems to be the nature of a push rather than a pull. And thus we begin to attribute to animals something more than a mere set of needs... namely some kind of internal motivation.[8]

This overlapping of biological needs also applies to humans — recall the earlier discussion of need hierarchies in chapter 3. But in humans this overlapping is far more complex since humans live enmeshed in a variety of systems, each of which affects the perception and fulfillment of needs, goals, and a sense of purpose.

Aside from biological and ecological systems, the other systems in which people live are formed by groups of people. These systems have their own needs, as discussed at length in chapter 3. They must organize activities within and across system boundaries so that the balance of input, the system's processing of inputs, and output is sufficient to ensure the system's survival. As with individuals, these needs become drives for the system so that goals are attained and the system's purpose is thereby fulfilled. A social work agency can be used as an illustration. The agency has to have economic resources, adequate staff, users of services, and a societal mandate in order to survive. People are recruited into a variety of positions/roles in order to meet these needs — administrators, direct service providers, secretaries, clients, and so on. Each is willing to help the agency meet its needs so that his or her own needs can also be met — these needs may be for income, social work services, a sense of importance, and so on. As the agency is successful in meeting its needs, its goals are attained — namely, to provide specific types of services to people, operate efficiently, use effective service delivery strategies, keep its employees and users happy, and so forth. In turn, its purpose is also achieved — it has become a significant part of the social welfare system. We can see, then, that needs, drives, and purposes motivate systems at all levels.

Needs are not constant. They represent a dynamic interplay between various components of the system as well as reflect human diversity variables such as ethnicity, sex, age, class, and so on. The social worker must be able to assess the intensity of the need as perceived by the system. Much behavior diagnosed as pathological results from systems being frustrated in their efforts to fulfill basic needs. Other maladaptive behaviors have their roots in discrepancies between the perceived needs from various parts of the social system. The adolescent's need for freedom and autonomy in decision making may conflict with parental needs for authority and acting protectively. The hospital organization's need for cost effective health care measures may influence the quality of service to the individual patient. The literature on organizational theory is full of examples of how the needs of the organization often take precedence over the needs of the expected beneficiary of organizational services.[9] The dilemma this poses for the social worker is obvious.

Adaptation, Coping, and Need Fulfillment

Awareness of needs and the ability to meet them are not always linked. Systems — including, of course, individuals as systems — sometimes encounter difficulty when attempting to meet their needs. When this occurs, two responses are common. One is *adaptation*, in which a system attempts to modify its behavior or its environment in order to meet its needs.[10] For example, people seeking the social approval of others may change their *reference group*, or the group with which they identify[11] from a disapproving to an approving one. Similarly, an organization may change its purpose if the environment changes in such a way as to make its original purpose no longer meaningful. The March of Dimes is a case in point. This organization shifted its purpose from fund raising for medical research about tuberculosis to research on respiratory diseases in general, once cures for tuberculosis were developed. A second response to need-meeting is *coping*, or developing an overall plan of action for overcoming stresses which is based on rationality, flexibility, and farsightedness.[12] Coping, therefore, commonly involves direct action as well as thought and emotion.[13] Coping is most accurately seen as one type of adaptation. Adaptation itself encompasses other responses as well which may not have the degree of rationality and flexibility that characterizes coping. For example, there are biological processes of adaptation that are not under one's conscious control — adrenalin production when frightened, or long-term genetic evolution, for instance. In contrast, coping is always a strategy selected by a system to deal with a need. The ability to cope and adapt is extremely important for systems if they are to meet their needs. Coping and adapting can involve, as we saw above, either system or environmental change. The latter is often a more efficient response to needs that may be experienced by a large number of people/systems. Here again we see the constant interplay of people and environment:

> When an active independent individual is forced into a role of passivity and dependency; or a submissive, sensitive primarily responsive person is expected to operate in a position in which he should be resourceful, have initiative and be aggressive, both will feel they are in the wrong places with respect to their most basic tendencies.[14]

An historical dimension is also an important part of the perception and fulfillment of needs. Needs are perceived differently at different points in time. Humankind no longer responds by adapting primarily to biological evolution; it has become increasingly involved as active participants in cultural evolution, especially in terms of technological development. Exciting as this may seem, it is not without problems. Gilula and Daniels warn: "In this new era, culture changes so rapidly that even time has assumed another dimension — the dimension of acceleration."[15] In our own lifetime many of us have observed vast technological changes in the media, the transportation industry, the ability to limit birth, and so forth. We have at the same time witnessed the impact of these changes on our social and cultural institutions.

The ability to control and limit birth, as a case in point, exemplifies how technology impacts on one's perception of life goals. One does not have to be especially astute historically to conclude that the position of women in Western civilization has been predominantly one of subjugation. Evidence abounds in the economic, religious, and family institutions to support this view. Yet the life chances of today's woman differ significantly from those of her mother and grandmother, thereby altering her perceptions of life goals and the avenues available to her in pursuing them. While it is an oversimplification to attribute the advent of "the pill" and the improvement and distribution of other forms of contraception as the single causative agent in this cultural change, its impact is without question. Today's woman is theoretically free to entertain multiple alternatives in charting her life goals — for example, alternatives in career choices, whether to marry or not to marry, to have children or not. This is not to imply that cultural institutions support each choice equally. In fact, quite the reverse is true as was pointed out in our discussions on human diversity. To choose to have a baby out of wedlock, or to engage in lesbian relationships incurs strong negative cultural sanctions. New institutional patterns are, however, emerging to support alternate life choices. Support systems such as those observed in gay and lesbian communities, among single parents, and/or among divorced people provide an opportunity for populations discriminated against to develop new types of resources.

Historical patterns are influenced not only by technological in novations (such as "the pill") but by cultural innovation. The turbulent decade of the sixties saw American society questioning the fundamental assumptions underlying many of its major social institutions — the economic system, the family system, the religious-ideological system. Perhaps the sixties did not deliver its promises in terms of radical institutional changes, but many of its "survivors" now perceive their life goals in a new light. Even though minority populations continue to experience exploitation in terms of institutional sexism, racism, and ageism, their position has improved somewhat as a result of the Civil Rights movement. At an individual level, these benefits have direct impacts on perceptions of one's life goals and the resources available to one in pursuing them. What we see is the changing nature of the perception of human needs as related to life goals along an historical continuum. Just as contemporary women enjoy new and expanding vistas in considering their life goals, so too are Blacks, Native Americans, the physically handicapped, the aged, and gay and lesbian populations perceiving new opportunities to identify and attain their life goals.

Information and Goal-Directed Behavior

Information is basic to our efforts to achieve our goals[16] but it is not in itself sufficient. We must first know what our goals are and then what information is relevant for our efforts to attain them. Formulating goals for ourselves results from the nature of our location in systems and our human diversity characteristics. If we live in a poor family our economic goals may be very limited because of our lack of resources. If we live in a Chicano family our goals may revolve around our relationships with our kin network rather than economic achievement. If we live in prison our goals may be focused on individual survival and personal integrity.[17] While there are indeed common human needs, understanding how these are translated into goals is highly dependent on system and human diversity variables. We should also note that individual goals are subsumed into goals of larger systems such as organizations and communities. System and human diversity variables are equally important at these levels.

Once goals have been formulated, we can put available information to better use[18] but here, too, systems and human diversity are critical variables. Systems differ in their need for and use of information. Organizations typically generate and use massive amounts of highly specific, objective data as part of their operation. Kinship systems generally use much less and far more subjective information. Individuals often rely on their actual firsthand experiences. These differences in system approaches to information can create difficult problems in exchanges between systems. A social service agency may require personal data that family members may consider inappropriate — or may not even have. Conversely, a hospital may overload a patient with more information than he or she wants, will use, or understands. In this case most of the information will probably be discarded, though the hospital may assume it is being used.[19] There is tremendous variation in the way diverse groups approach information. Some value scientific information and use it routinely for decision making. Others trust to personal judgments, and still others rely on spiritual beliefs. Each approach produces useable information. The way in which it can be used is quite different, but becomes an integral part of the group's culture and structure.

Identifying needs and developing strategies to meet them depends on information. As noted earlier, people's perceptions develop as part of their psychological development. Although based on biological characteristics, perceptual ability is developed socially and becomes selective in that people learn to perceive what their group values and considers important. This same process tends to operate in larger systems as well, since they reflect the interests of their members. The use of information in the process of meeting needs is, therefore, highly variable. There is no one reality — it is socially constructed and varies between groups.[20] Once reality is created it becomes a *self-fulfilling prophecy*, meaning that people usually arrange their environments* to create the reality that their social group considers important.[22] For example, people prejudiced against Blacks will interpret their behavior as unacceptable — their clothes are too brightly colored, their smiles are indicative of lack of seriousness, and so forth. People who are not prejudiced would interpret these behaviors quite differently, perhaps as reflective of cultural attitudes toward personal pride and caring for others.

As we have already seen, information about the environment is an important variable in perceived needs. Groups that are systematically disadvantaged often see the environment as hostile. Needs revolving around self-protection may then become dominant and serve to restrict the group's efforts to explore parts of the environment that might offer more resources. When this happens we can see two self-fulfilling prophecies. The dominant group's definition of the minority group as passive and limited in abilities is fulfilled; the minority group's definition of the environment as limiting is also fulfilled. The way information has been processed in this example therefore turns out to be a significant part of the way needs and the life goals which flow from them are negotiated between the two groups. This serves to illustrate the close link between information, needs, and goals.

---

*It is useful here to remember that environment has two components: "(1) The *objective environment* that exists independently of the person's perception of it; and (2) the *subjective environment* as it is perceived and reported by the person."[21] Both are extremely important.

Goal-Directed Behavior and Social Work Practice

The importance of the goal-directed behavior perspective for practice is its focus on purpose. Human behavior generally is not random.[23] People act as they do because they are attempting to meet their needs as they perceive them. These needs then provide the drive and motivation for them to engage in specific behaviors that will help them achieve the goals that flow from the needs. Remember, however, that reality differs based on one's perception. In extreme cases, mentally ill people create fantasies that cause them to perceive the environment in a way that is totally different from the environment as it is perceived by most others. The needs which result from such perceptions can lead to death rather than health — nutritional needs as perceived by people who suffer from anorexia (the fear of eating) is a case in point.

For most people, however, differences in perception are only a matter of degree. Here again an understanding of human diversity is essential for social workers. Without it differences in people's perceptions of needs and goals are judged against the standards of the viewer. This use of one's own values and perceptions to judge those of others is called *ethnocentrism*,[24] and leads to seeing the behavior of others as illogical and irrelevant simply because it is different from one's own. Social work practice demands the opposite view, that all behavior can be understood as purposeful if we consider it within its own context — recall the dual perspective idea. That is not to say that all behavior must necessarily be accepted and encouraged. It is the social worker's responsibility to help people to function more effectively. Behavior that is destructive to oneself or others must be analyzed with the people involved so that alternatives can be considered. In some cases, societal prohibitions are so strong that behavior is simply not permissible regardless of its cultural context — poisoning someone, for example. In these cases, social workers have a moral responsibility to support societal norms.

In most cases, however, social workers mediate between people's perceptions and their environments. Workers who feel that elements in their work place endanger their health perceive a situation that prevents their fulfilling the basic need of physical survival. The social worker can help the workers negotiate with their employer so that their needs are met more effectively — or so they are given access to information that will help them change their perception, if appropriate. The important point is that social workers believe that most people can be trusted to engage in behavior that is purposeful given their perception of reality. As Germain notes, assessment of a situation must be made by those seeking to solve the problem.[25] Once this attitude is adopted, it is easier to see that behavior which at first glance may look illogical is perfectly sensible given that person's experienced reality. Shopping in a small neighborhood grocery where prices are higher than in a nearby supermarket may not make sense unless one realizes that the smaller store will extend credit and the larger one won't. For poor people who can expect to have periods when they have little or no money, shopping where credit is available makes sense. Also, the smaller store may be more responsive to requests to stock food items preferred by particular cultural groups.[26]

In their own way, most people engage in some approximation of the problem-solving process that social workers use in their practice:[27] defining the problem, assessing resources and obstacles, selecting a plan, carrying out the plan, and assessing results. Their use of this process is often very informal and, as noted earlier, the kind of information used may be very selective. Nevertheless, their behavior is systematic and goal-directed. It is the responsibility of social workers to help people use the problem-solving process more effectively, rather than to undermine their efforts to do so. Most people want to understand and meet their needs in the most effective way possible so that they can achieve their life goals. As social workers become more skilled at understanding the context within which people from diverse groups function, they can maximize their helpfulness to people.

Conclusion: Professional Mission and Life Goals

Social work as a profession committed to enhancing person-environment transactions must recognize and constructively deal with the internal and external barriers to problem solving that influence people's efforts to act in purposeful, goal-directed ways. Fundamental to all successful problem solving is the assumption that the resources needed to achieve its goals are available to the system. Social work has traditionally responded to unmet needs by providing resources through an interlocking network of social welfare programs, policies, and services. The assumption underlying such an approach to societal provision is that individuals, groups, and communities will be able to better achieve their purposes if provided with sufficient resources. As this chapter has pointed out, however, the needs of members of particular groups are often frustrated in favor of the needs of the larger social system. If, in fact, the profession is to address people-environment transactions, it is important to question the fundamental assumptions underlying social provision. If social-structural variables inhibit the individual from realizing his or her life goals, professional purpose must mandate social action to remove the obstacles. When the goals of various components of the system are in conflict the profession must advocate on behalf of the exploited populations.

Addressing human behavior content in this light illustrates the interrelated nature of the human behavior and social policy components of the social work curriculum. Do the goals of the profession accelerate or impede the goal-directed behavior of individuals, groups, and communities? The concluding chapters will address the value of policy related questions raised by human behavior content and present a working framework for "pulling it all together."

Study Questions

1. Break the class into several groups, each with an optimum membership of five or six. Each group is to represent a component of the school system: students, teachers, parents, and so on. Identify the primary purposes of the component to which you belong. Discuss how these purposes conflict or reinforce the purposes of the other components of the system.

2. One perceives life goals based on the alternatives provided by the culture in which one lives. What alternatives does contemporary American culture provide for women in terms of career choices? How do these differ from options available for men? How do they differ from the alternatives available to women twenty-five years ago?

3. What is meant by the statement made in this chapter that subcultures assigned a "deviant" status by the dominant culture often use this status as an opportunity to turn obstacles into resources? Give examples.

4. Transactions between people and their social environment seek to meet the needs of both. Discuss coping mechanisms as problem-solving approaches to achieving a comfortable fit between people and environments.

5. Social work as a profession is committed to removing barriers to the maximum functioning of individuals, groups, and communities. How do these barriers impact on the purposeful behavior of the individual, the group, and the community? How do barriers in turn affect life goals?

Notes

1. Charlotte Towle, *Common Human Needs*, rev. ed. (New York: National Association of Social Workers, 1965), p. 18.

2. D. B. Klein, *A History of Scientific Psychology* (New York: Basic Books, 1970), p. 49.

3. Ann Templeton Brownlee, *Community, Culture, and Care* (St. Louis: C. V. Mosby, 1978).

4. Alfred Baldwin, *Theories of Child Development* (New York: John Wiley, 1968), pp. 409 ff.

5. Ibid., p. 459.

6. George S. Klein, *Perception, Motives, and Personality* (New York: Alfred A. Knopf, 1970), pp. 73–79.

7.   Margaret Boden, *Purposive Explanation in Psychology* (Cambridge, Mass.: Harvard University Press, 1972), p. 25.

8.   Karl Menninger, *The Vital Balance: The Life Process in Mental Health and Illness* (New York: Viking Press, 1963), p. 108.

9.   See, for example, Esther Stanton, *Clients Come Last* (Beverly Hills, Ca.: Sage, 1970).

10. Marshall Gilula and David Daniels, "Violence and Man's Struggle to Adapt," in Adela S. Baer, ed., *Heredity and Society* (New York: Macmillan, 1973), p. 134.

11. Grace Ganter and Margaret Yeakel, *Human Behavior and the Social Environment* (New York: Columbia University Press, 1980), p.45.

12. Aaron Antonovsky, *Health, Stress, and Coping* (San Francisco: Jossey-Bass, 1979), p. 112.

13. Alan Monat and Richard Lazarus, *Stress and Coping* (New York: Columbia University Press, 1977), pp. 8–9.

14. Charlotte Buhler, "Theoretical Observations About Life's Basic Tendencies," *American Journal of Psychopathology*, 13 (1955): 563.

15. Gilula and Daniels, pp. 132–153.

16. P. R. Day, *Methods of Learning Communication Skills* (Oxford: Pergamon Press, 1977), pp. 1–25.

17. See Susan Sheehan, *A Prison and a Prisoner*(Boston: Houghton Mifflin, 1978).

18. Sidney E. Zimbalist, *Historic Themes and Landmarks in Social Welfare Research* (New York: Harper & Row, 1977), pp. 3–27.

19. Brownlee, pp. 215–242.

20. Peter Berger and Thomas Luckmann, *The Social Construction of Reality* (New York: Doubleday, 1966).

21. John French, Jr., Willard Rogers, and Sidney Cobb, "Adjustment as Person-Environment Fit," in George V. Coelho, David Hamburg, and John E. Adams, eds., *Coping and Adaptation* (New York: Basic Books, 1974), p. 316.

22. W. I. Thomas, "The Definition of the Situation" and Robert Merton, "The Self-Fulfilling Prophecy," in Lewis Coser, ed., *The Pleasures of Sociology* (New York: Merton Books, 1980), pp. 26–47.

23. George Coelho and John Adams, "Introduction," in Coelho, Hamburg, Adams, pp. XIX–XXII.

24.   Ronald C. Federico, *Sociology*, 2nd ed. (Reading, Mass.: Addison-Wesley, 1979), pp. 45–46.

25.   Content from a workshop led by Dr. Carel Germain for The Council on Social Work Education in New York City, February 14, 1980.

26.   See Susan Sheehan, *A Welfare Mother* (New York: Saturday Review Press, 1975).

27.   Ronald C. Federico, *The Social Welfare Institution*, 3rd ed. (Lexington, Mass.: D. C. Heath, 1980), pp. 159–160.

Additional Readings

Berelson, Bernard, and Steiner, Gary A. *Human Behavior: An Inventory of Scientific Findings*. New York: Harcourt, Brace and World, 1967.
Bolles, Robert C. *Theory of Motivation*. 2nd edition. New York: Harper & Row, 1975.
Bronfenbrenner, Urie and Mahoney, Maureen A., eds. *Influences on Human Development*. 2nd ed. Hinsdale, Ill.: Dryden Press, 1975.
Buchler, Charlotte and Massarik, eds. *The Course of Human Life: A Study of Goals in the Humanistic Perspective*. New York: Springer Publisher, 1968.
Cofer, Charles N. *Motivation and Emotion*. Glenville, Ill.: Scott, Foresman, 1972.
Greenberg, Harold. *Social Environment and Behavior*. Cambridge, Mass.: Schenkman Publishing Co., 1971.
Maslow, Abraham. *The Farther Reaches of Human Nature*. New York: University of Kentucky Press, 1971.
Monat, Alan and Lazarus, Richard S., eds. *Stress and Coping: An Anthology*. New York: Columbia University Press, 1977.
Rosenblueth, Arturo; Wiener, Nobert; and Bigelow, Julian. "Behavior, Purpose and Teleology." In *Modern Systems Research for the Behavioral Scientist*, edited by Walter Buckley, pp. 221–225. Chicago: Aldine Publishing, 1968.
Russell, Wallace A., ed. *Milestones in Motivation: Contributions to the Psychology of Drive and Purpose*. Englewood Cliffs, N. J.: Prentice-Hall, 1970.
Stein, Herman D., and Cloward, Richard A., eds. *Social Perspectives on Behavior*. New York: Free Press, 1961.

PART III

Applying Concepts to Practice Situations

CHAPTER 5

An Integrated View of the Life Cycle

Introduction

So far this book has developed three basic perspectives useful for integrating and applying knowledge in order to better achieve the purposes of social work. These three perspectives are systems, human diversity, and goal-directed behavior, and throughout there has been an effort to apply each to practice situations. The book's final chapters will address the task of developing and applying a framework based on these ideas to help us understand the situations social workers routinely encounter in their practice. This chapter uses the framework to analyze the life cycle, and includes a definition and discussion of the life cycle and its importance for social work practice. This is followed by the development of a framework to use in analyzing major life cycle stages. Finally, the framework is applied and related to social work practice. Chapter 6 provides a concluding integration of the book's content by returning to the central concept of professional purpose.

Defining the Life Cycle

The concept of the *life cycle* is an easy one to understand. It simply refers to the period from conception to death, encompassing the totality of the physical, psychological, social-structural, and cultural experiences of living. By its very nature, the life cycle is an integrating concept, since it looks at the parallel development of biological and social functioning. While the concept itself is a simple one to grasp, there have been a variety of approaches to identifying its component parts. Some have been confined to one discipline, such as the biological view of the development of the organism through the life cycle. Others have attempted to at least in part relate biological and social functioning to one another — many psychological theories are examples. In practice, however, virtually all life cycle theories have emphasized one particular aspect of human development — usually either the psychological or biological — and have given particular emphasis to certain points during the life cycle — most commonly infancy through adolescence.

This chapter will take a somewhat different approach. It will emphasize the developmental tasks that characterize human life and look at these tasks as they are performed at different points in the life cycle. This task approach will then be used to tie biological, psychological, social-structural, and cultural variables together. The idea of *life cycle stages* will be used to refer to relatively arbitrarily selected points associated with certain chronological ages. They are convenient concepts to use in talking about different points in the life cycle at which biological and social forces can be examined. Others might select other stages, but this is less important than the kind of analysis that is done at whatever the stages selected are.

Life Stages.   In this chapter the following life stages will be used: conception and birth, infancy and early childhood (from birth to about 4), middle and late childhood (from about 4 to about 12), adolescence (from about 13 to about 18), young adulthood (from about 18 to about 25), middle adulthood (from about 25 to about 45), late adulthood (from about 45 to about 61), retirement (from about 62 to death), and death itself. These stages are defined as they are for purely illustrative and analytical reasons. They do not represent any universals in human life, since the life cycle can be ended at any point and since there are wide cultural variations in definitions of life stages. Probably the only universals are conception and death. What occurs between these two stages can vary from miscarriage (death before birth), to death at birth, to death at any point up through advanced old age.

Life Tasks.   The principal significance of life cycle stages is the way each emphasizes particular life tasks that are necessary for human development. Life tasks are defined by cultures and translated through social structures into specific expected behaviors. For example, in childhood there are cultural expectations pertaining to toilet training. These range from rigid expectations of when toilet training should be accomplished to very relaxed perspectives about its importance. Cultural beliefs such as these are then translated into appropriate behaviors. Examples of this behavior are the procedures used to teach toilet training at the appropriate time. If the child accomplishes this task at the appropriate time he or she is rewarded with praise, while children who take longer generate worry for their parents and often suffer some type of punishment. In societies where toilet training is not accorded so much importance children may simply become trained when they are ready to emulate adult behavior. Very little attention to the process is likely to be paid by others. So, while becoming toilet trained is a universal life task, it is approached very differently by different societies. There is, of course, no "right" approach to this task, but instead a variety of approaches that various cultures find acceptable.

Toilet training is a good example to use in pointing out some interesting characteristics of life tasks, namely, that they have biological components, they have social-structural components, and they have lifelong significance. Let us look at each in turn.

Biological Components of Life Tasks. The societal definitions of what life tasks are include some degree of recognition of biological realities. For example, no society expects a six-week-old infant to be toilet trained because it is a physiological impossibility. Similarly, men can not be expected to bear children, although they may be expected to play a significant role in nurturing a child. We have already seen that sometimes societal definitions override biological reality, however. This can happen in the case of life tasks. For example, sexual intercourse between men and women is defined by the dominant group in the United States as appropriate only in marriage. This is in turn defined as a task of adulthood. Since the biological ability to be sexually active occurs much earlier, society's definition often builds in problems with this life task. In general, however, societal definitions of life tasks attempt to relate biological capacity to preferred social behavior.

Social Structural Components of Life Tasks. Life tasks serve two principal social-structural purposes. The first is *human development*. The challenges of life tasks stimulate the interaction between people and the environment so that genetically inherited capacities can be developed. In attempting to master learning tasks, for example, the child develops his or her cognitive capacity while also developing a psychological sense of self — hopefully as a competent person who can successfully manage the everyday environment. The child also learns how to relate to others through seeking help, getting rewarded, and so forth. This human development task is closely related to the second — *meeting social needs.* As noted earlier, society as a whole and in its subsystems seeks some level of structural stability in those activities necessary to maintain the structure. People need to have enough food to live; reproduction must occur; children have to be cared for; behavior which harms oneself or others has to be controlled. These major societal needs spawn the complex social structure discussed earlier, consisting of norms, positions, roles, social institutions, and so on. If these are seriously challenged or break down, the whole structure is in jeopardy. Therefore, society defines life tasks in ways that prepare and encourage people to carry out needed societal functions. Children do not only need to develop their learning capacity for themselves, or as part of their own human development, but in order to be able to participate in the structures of society. People are expected to marry not only for love, but also in order to create a structure for orderly reproduction and child care. The social-structural components of life tasks, then, attempt to provide for both human development and societal needs.

Life Tasks throughout the Life Cycle. As we will see in more detail later in this chapter, specific life tasks differ at each life cycle stage. This reflects in part changing biological needs and capacities. However, it is also true that certain basic life tasks remain with us throughout the life cycle — what changes is our method of addressing them. Throughout the life cycle we have to meet our basic physical needs. As children we rely on others, as adults we attempt to be independent, and as elderly people we may have to find some balance between dependence and independence. Similarly, the task of relating to others is accomplished differently at each stage of the life cycle, but remains a lifelong task. We can also look at the tasks of securing a sense of psychological well-being and environmental mastery in similar ways.

The basic point is that some life tasks cut across the life cycle and others are unique to particular life stages. For example, we generally learn to speak during the stage of early childhood. However, early childhood is also a time in which relationships are established with significant others outside the family, such as peers or adults in organized settings like nursery schools and stores. This task is one which continues throughout life, although the ways it is performed change. Yet even this simple example is indicative of the complexity of human behavior generated by human diversity. While we learn to speak in early childhood, we may learn to speak additional languages at other points in the life cycle. Some people even have to relearn how to speak if their vocal chords are damaged through illness or accident. Some deaf people only learn to speak long after childhood when their deafness is better understood and appropriate surgical and/or educational resources are available, although they may have learned to communicate through sign language or writing as children. It cannot be emphasized enough that human behavior in specific situations must be carefully analyzed within the context of human diversity. Any attempt to speak generally about human behavior during the life cycle inevitably omits much of the richness of human diversity. Life stages are simply devices to help us identify the ways human life becomes a totality comprising of biological, psychological, social-structural, and cultural factors. They should not be seen as rigid, universal, unilineal stages clearly separate from each other.

Resources and Obstacles

Resources and obstacles have been discussed in previous chapters. Now they need to be reviewed in relationship to life stages. As one progresses through life, one has access to changing resources and confronts different obstacles. Together, resources and obstacles affect the *ease* with which life tasks are performed as well as the *way* they are performed. Resources and obstacles change because of biological and social-structural factors. A child's bright red hair and freckles often attract praise, yet in an adult these features may be seen as too conspicuous and hence undesirable. Thus looks will be very different resources and obstacles at different points in the life cycle. Multiple sclerosis in a child may elicit caring and concern, but may be the cause of rejection and social isolation for an adult who is expected to be independent. Similar examples can be found for all of the biological sources of human diversity explored in chapter 3. Biological variables in interaction with societal expectations keep changing, leading to very different combinations of resources and obstacles.

One way to approach the idea of resources and obstacles throughout the life cycle is to identify the elements of both which may exist in the same situation. Thus a businesswoman considered to be very attractive may face conflicting responses to her beauty in a business situation. Her appearance can be a resource in that she gets compliments which reinforce her sense of well-being, and is deferred to whenever colleagues open doors for her. Her appearance can also be an obstacle when she is ignored in business discussions because her colleagues consider her more decorative than competent, or when she is expected to grant sexual favors in return for recognition and rewards she has earned through her competence as a worker. Similarly, a man who is unemployed because of a disability incurred at work may have difficulty carrying out his roles as husband and father if his spouse and children resent his inability to provide economic support for the family. Yet his qualifying for medical and job retraining services through Workmen's Compensation may be an important resource for his being able to recover his roles as defined by his particular family unit. Obviously some resources are far more desirable than others, and some obstacles are far more limiting than others. Being wealthy is more often a resource than an obstacle, and having a handicap or illness more frequently an obstacle than a resource. Nevertheless, an adequate understanding of life cycle potential necessitates sensitivity to all of the ways behaviors have potential for being resources and obstacles in particular situations and at particular points in the life cycle.

A Framework for Analyzing the Life Cycle

The life cycle is an important context for social work practice. The relationship of societal demands and people's resources that characterizes each stage in the life cycle creates predictable needs and reasonably predictable responses to those needs. For example, in adulthood most people are especially concerned with their sense of accomplishment and the quality of their intimate relations with others. Thus it is very common for anxieties related to life purpose to arise during this period. Of course the specific needs that arise and the exact responses to them are strongly affected by human diversity factors. This is especially true for understanding resources and obstacles that vary from person to person and group to group. It is also the case that society's responses to difference determine whether something is defined as an obstacle or as a resource. For example, neighbors in an affluent suburb banding together to help a resident whose house has burned down are generally considered a resource. However, dominant groups may consider residents in a minority neighborhood who organize a rent strike to be an obstacle because of their efforts to challenge existing organizational structures. A social worker, of course, would probably assess resources and obstacles in these cases somewhat differently than others.

The following framework will be used to combine all of the aspects of human behavior discussed so far and to focus them on understanding behavior throughout the life cycle. The framework focuses on life tasks as defined biologically (obtaining life-sustaining nutrients as well as realizing biological capacities for growth and development), psychologically (accomplishing developmental and adaptive behaviors), social-structurally (meeting social expectations), and culturally (learning definitions of the appropriate). For each type of task, one looks for the relevant resources and obstacles. These are biological, psychological, social-structural, and cultural in nature, and reflect the systems, human diversity, and goal-directed perspectives discussed in earlier chapters.

It is not the purpose of this chapter to provide an exhaustive analysis of the life cycle. This chapter seeks instead to demonstrate how the framework presented above is used. When used properly, it provides the kind of holistic view of human behavior organized around life stages essential for social workers. Living is a constant interplay of biological, psychological, social-structural, and cultural forces working toward meeting individual, group, organizational, and societal goals. This fundamental interaction between people and the environment leads to behaviors that are perceived as help-ful or problematic. Such interaction is the focus of the profession of social work. Maintaining this focus requires the balanced, holistic view provided by the framework.

FIGURE 5.1

A Framework for Analyzing the Life Cycle

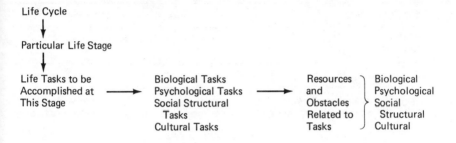

A Framework to Analyze Each Life Stage

In order to analyze each life stage, the life cycle framework pre-sented in figure 5.1 can be further broken down. Biological tasks would include such things as obtaining sufficient nutrients and pro-tection from physical abuse. In order to accomplish these tasks, biological resources would include proper nutrition and reflexes used in protecting oneself from physical threat. Obstacles would include substance abuse decreasing the desire to eat or affecting nutritional needs, and birth defects decreasing one's ability to pro-tect oneself in the environment. In other words, biological variables are those physiological characteristics that affect the needs of the biological system and the ability of the system (individual) to meet its needs through interaction with the environment.

Psychological variables are physiological characteristics and be-havioral patterns that affect the ability of the system (individual) to perceive, organize, and interact with the environment. Psychological tasks would include obtaining sufficient nurturance and compre-

FIGURE 5.2

A Framework for Analyzing Each Stage in the Life Cycle*

Human Diversity and Systems Variables	Tasks at this Life Cycle Stage	Factors Affecting *Ease* with Which and *Ways* in Which Tasks Attempted	
		Resources	Obstacles
BIOLOGICAL			
PSYCHOLOGICAL			
SOCIAL-STRUCTURAL			
CULTURAL			

*In this book, the following stages are used: conception and birth, infancy, childhood, adolescence, young adulthood, adulthood, late adulthood, retirement, and death.

hending the environment. Psychological resources include responsiveness to the behavior of others and high intelligence. Obstacles include rigid personality defenses that skew one's perception of the environment and learning disorders.

Social structures define life cycle tasks by generating social expectations and certain kinds of social arrangements. These impact on the structure of the human environment and its differential effects on various groups. For example, adults are generally expected to marry, and the elderly are supposed to withdraw from gainful employment so that younger people will have access to jobs. Social structures are created to support these expectations, and become resources to those who meet the expectations. For example, marriage ceremonies provide social, psychological, and monetary support to couples as they begin their married lives, and most elderly qualify for some sort of financial assistance. On the other hand, social structures can also be obstacles. The single person who chooses not to marry is denied a social ritual to support his or her choice, and is often stigmatized for not having met the social expectation of marriage. Similarly, an elderly person is penalized financially if he or she earns an income beyond the low levels set by public financial assistance programs.

Culture defines the values and beliefs underlying social-structural expectations of appropriate tasks at each stage in the life cycle. Social-structural arrangements generally reflect the culture of dominant groups. It is cultural beliefs that lead to particular kinds of marriage customs and ceremonies, for example, or even the expectation that an appropriate life task for adults is to marry. Cultural beliefs are resources in that they provide the value context for people's lives essential for their sense of identity and belongingness. However, they can be obstacles when they support beliefs and behaviors different from the dominant group's, as is often the case with minority cultures. For example, the Spanish language is a resource for Puerto Ricans in Puerto Rico but an obstacle in those parts of the United States mainland where Spanish is not commonly spoken.

The rest of this chapter will use the framework presented in figure 5.2 to analyze life stages very briefly. This will be done within the context of the life cycle framework in figure 5.1. Remember that the purpose of this analysis is *illustrative*. It should help the reader understand the framework better so that he or she can use it in later efforts to understand human behavior in its social context. This will be an important lifelong task for any social work practitioner. Rather than using specific references throughout the text, we have provided a basic bibliography for the life cycle at the end of the chapter. The material in the text represents our interpretation of content taken from a combination of these and other sources.

Conception and Birth as a Life Stage

Tasks.   Conception and birth is a period of expansion for individuals, groups, and society. For the individual (the parent), the self becomes a source of life for others. This generally adds to one's sense of competence, continuity, and importance, although it also increases one's responsibilities. For specific groups and for society as a whole, conception and birth ensure the survival of the social unit by replacing members and even increasing the size of the unit.

The focus during this life stage is on decision making and preparation for new life. The decision to have a child is a significant one for the individuals directly involved. It engages a network of interpersonal relationships that will be used to provide emotional and financial support during the pregnancy and after the child is born. Groups impinge on individual decision making through cultural definitions of the desirability of pregnancy and the conditions under which it should occur. Groups also form the support structures that provide the context in which conception and birth occur.

Biological tasks focus on the reproductive act and the physical and emotional conditions needed for a healthy pregnancy and a secure birth. Psychological tasks relate to the readiness of the people involved to conceive and carry a child. This includes a sense of well-being about oneself and the baby, knowledge about conception, pregnancy, and birth, and the existence of emotional support systems. Social-structural tasks pertain to the availability of an environment in which conception can occur by choice and the pregnancy and birth can occur in a safe context. Cultural tasks are those that engage belief and value systems to support the parents and the child. Together, these four task areas attempt to provide for the emotional and physical life-sustaining needs of the child and its parents. This includes the creation of a receptive social context in which the child will be able to grow and develop.

The life stage including conception and birth is unique in that, during it, the person being conceived and born is almost completely dependent on others. Conception itself is the result of decisions and actions by others which precede the person-to-be. The conditions under which the fetus develops are also strongly influenced by others, especially the biological parents. The task of the fetus itself — to develop physically and survive — is engaged through its genetically inherited developmental potential. Nevertheless, for the fetus the task is almost exclusively a physiological one. The social, psychological, and cultural factors involved relate to the other people involved in the environment of the fetus. The biological mother is, of course, of particular importance. Even the birth process is heavily affected by others. The fetus has its own physiological tasks to perform in the birth process, but the environment into which the fetus emerges is determined by others. For example, even if a doctor diagnosed that a Caesarean section would be needed for a safe delivery the parents would have to initiate the decisions and actions to make it possible.

This life stage is a good example of the fact that the tasks faced by individuals at various life cycle stages affect each other. The task of the fetus is to grow and survive, though the likelihood of this happening is strongly influenced by the life stage tasks of the biological parents. Are the parents unmarried adolescents or financially secure married adults, who may even already have other children? The readiness of biological parents to see a fetus through pregnancy, birth, and infancy is an important influence on the new person's ability to carry out his or her own life tasks. Although this point is easy to see at the life stage of conception and birth, it is true throughout the life cycle. In adulthood, the way in which one's sense of accomplishment and satisfaction develops (tasks at that stage) is influenced by the way in which one's children have progressed through infancy, childhood, and adolescence, or the way one's own parents have handled the life tasks associated with retirement and death. Throughout the remainder of this chapter the emphasis will be on the life tasks facing the individual encountering the life cycle stage being discussed. Nevertheless, you should keep in mind the ways in which the interaction between life cycle stages influences the performance of life tasks throughout the life cycle.

Resources.   Biological resources are those which increase the probability that the mother and child will be healthy. These include the mother's age at conception, her previous pregnancy history, her health, and whether she is addicted to any substances. In general, women between the ages of about 16 and 35 run the least risk of complications during pregnancy. Women who are healthy — that is, who are disease-free and receive proper nutrition — who have not had pregnancy difficulties in the past, and who are not dependent on any drugs or narcotics are least likely to encounter biological difficulties during pregnancy. The age, nutritional level, and health of the father are also relevant to the biological processes of conception and pregnancy. Finally, the genetic composition of both parents is an important determinant of the course of a pregnancy and birth.

Psychological resources are those which help parents decide whether they wish to have a child and whether they have the emotional and financial means to do so. This includes knowledge about parenthood, conception, pregnancy, and birth — knowledge basic to informed decision making that will ultimately relate to one's sense of readiness for parenthood. Personality variables are also important. A sense of personal well-being and strength and the ability to confront new situations help people adjust to the demands of pregnancy and parenthood. Willingness to share with others and the ability to cope effectively with physical and emotional stress are also helpful.

Social-structural resources are those factors that provide concrete help for pregnant women and new parents, as well as social-structural conditions that serve to validate one's changed identity as a parent. Tax benefits for children, health insurance to pay for the medical costs of pregnancy and birth, and employee policies that allow a woman to take leaves during pregnancy are all significant resources. Additional social-structural resources include the quality of medical care available, social rituals such as baby showers that allow family and friends to indicate their support, the availability of information about conception and parenthood, and personal and genetic counseling. There is a direct relationship between minority group membership and the availability of these socioeconomic resources. Social-structural resources are generally more available to the non-poor, which usually means to members of the dominant groups.

Cultural resources are those that provide group approval for conception and birth and that provide a knowledge context for these activities. Being the proper age and marital status as defined by one's own group places one's pregnancy in an acceptable value framework that will lead to social praise and support. Using socially acceptable means of prenatal care, following prescribed sex role behaviors, and involving appropriate others, such as parents and siblings, also generally encourage cultural beliefs and values in support of conception, pregnancy, and birth. Of course, however, each cultural group has its own definitions of whether conception is desirable, and if so, how it should be managed.

Obstacles. As we saw in the earlier discussion of resources and obstacles, obstacles are those factors that increase the biological and psychological risks of conception and birth and detach people from the usual social-structural and cultural supports at this life stage. Biological obstacles would include a woman being very young or old at conception, or having a history of pregnancy complications. Other biological obstacles would include the incidence of a disease such as VD in either parent, substance dependency by the mother, or the existence of genetically transmitted problems in either parent. Psychological obstacles might be having to adjust to an unwanted child or very limited knowledge of conception, pregnancy, and birth. Another psychological obstacle would be feelings of severe inadequacy by either parent in terms of their new parenting responsibilities.

Examples of social-structural obstacles would be inadequate financial resources to pay for necessary medical treatment or to provide proper nutrition for the mother, abusive physical conditions which threaten the mother's biological and emotional well-being, and medical technology that is inadequate for the mother's needs — a factor that is especially important if there is a complication during pregnancy or at birth. Additional social-structural obstacles would include lack of information about conception, pregnancy, and parenthood and the unavailability of counseling to help parents decide whether conception is a wise choice or if pregnancy should be terminated. As noted earlier, poverty is directly related to physical well-being. Therefore, biological and social-structural resources/obstacles are closely associated, since poverty results from economic, political, and human diversity variables. Cultural obstacles are those beliefs and values that devalue conception and birth. Usually this occurs only for certain categories of people. For example, unmarried women may be considered unfit to bear children. Another example is when a dominant group denigrates conception among members of minority groups, such as when white Americans fear that Black Americans have too many children. In both of these examples, obstacles discourage conception or make the conception, pregnancy, and birth processes more problematic biologically or socially than need be.

Implications for Social Work.   Conceiving a child is a major life event. For many it involves a major decision that requires as much information and emotional support as possible. It is often a decision shared with significant others, such as family and friends, who can be critical elements in the decision. For some, conception is not decided, it simply happens. This often reflects lack of information about basic physiological processes. In other cases, conception is considered a natural part of life and accepted whenever it occurs. And for still others, it is a decision made to achieve other goals such as a sense of intimacy with another, a feeling of personal importance, or a feeling of independence. The social worker has to be able to disentangle the many factors that may be involved in conception in order to provide appropriate resources.

Pregnancy is a time of physical and emotional changes and adjustments. The pregnant woman needs as much information as possible about her pregnancy and a great deal of support as she adjusts her activities and emotions to it. Many women also need financial, housing, and other supports so that adequate nutrition and physical care are available. Others involved in the pregnancy, especially the father, also need to be supported and informed. When the pregnancy threatens to lead to exclusion from supporting social structures — such as school, family, work, and so on — efforts should be made to strengthen these linkages or find alternatives. The existence of conditions that threaten the physical well-being of the mother or child — such as addiction, disease, illness, or genetic factors — demands a thorough analysis of their implications so that appropriate action can be taken. When physically or psychologically needed and culturally acceptable, abortion is a potential resource to be considered.

The birth process is often approached with fear and uncertainty. This frequently reflects lack of information and fear of pain. It may also reflect anxiety over medical costs or disagreement with the medical procedures most commonly used in hospitals. Alternative places and methods of delivery should be explored in order to find those most compatible with a particular person's situation and background. Planning for the care of the newborn infant is also important, especially in cases where the mother may be alone, lack resources, be ill, or be ambivalent about her pregnancy.

There are a host of concerns that social workers can anticipate at this life stage. As we have seen, the needs for information, for physical and medical care, for help in decision making, and for solidifying linkages with support systems are especially critical. In addition, basic life-sustaining resources may be needed, such as money, food, and shelter. The fact that this life stage usually leads to alterations in established life patterns often creates the need for counseling in one or more of the multiple systems that may be involved. For many people, creating new life is a happy, exciting adventure. For others it is quite routine. Still others approach it with fear, anxiety, and a sense of desperation. A social worker must be able to anticipate and respond to all these possibilities so that the newly conceived person can have the best possible chance of meeting the basic task at this life stage — physical development and survival.

Infancy and Early Childhood as a Life Stage

Tasks.   As defined here, infancy and early childhood make up the period from birth to about four years of age. Infancy is a period that involves the infant as well as those around it, and so the tasks at this life stage reflect this range of people. Generally, infancy is a period of growth. The child gradually matures biologically, gaining more and more mastery over his or her own limbs, bodily functions, perceptual organs, communication mechanisms, emotional states, and relationships with others. Part of these accomplishments occur through the development of language. The infant's parents also grow, responding to new demands on their time, energy, and emotions. Their relationships with each other — if there are two of them — are modified, as well as their interactions with other family members, friends, and social institutions. For the infant, then, the major task is to develop biologically, psychologically, and socially. For the parents the task is to find new life patterns and satisfactions through parenthood, and to protect and nurture the new member of society so it will be able ultimately to become a productive participant in the social structure.

Resources. Biological resources of the infant are its genetic endowments. Capacities in the form of reflexes, brain characteristics, neurological mechanisms, skeletal structure, and basic organic health make it possible for the infant to gradually perceive, organize, and master its environment. The degree of development and mastery will, of course, reflect the nature of the child's genetic equipment. An infant's physical attractiveness, as defined culturally, is also an important biological resource. For the parents, biological resources would encompass their own physical well-being and their ability to perceive and handle the infant. Psychological resources in the infant are closely tied to biological endowments. However, the interaction between biological needs and the social environment is extremely important, with psychological resources emerging as a result of it. An infant whose needs are met consistently and promptly will usually develop personality resources that increase the probability of continued growth and strength. Social and physical stimulation will enable the infant to develop its perceptual and cognitive capacities, as well as its ability to relate happily to others. Parents' resources include their knowledge of parenting and infant development, their ability to adapt to the new demands on them imposed by the infant, and their sense of competence which enables them to undertake the often difficult and uncertain activities involved in child-rearing.

Social-structural resources for the infant are those structures which enhance its survival and its growth efforts. The family — broadly defined, not just in terms of the intact family — is obviously of critical importance. The nature of the medical care available, neighborhood resources that relate to the adequacy of housing, nutrition, physical security, interpersonal relationships, and child care facilities are also examples of important social-structural resources. These resources are also important for the parents, although theirs might also include the availability of education about child-rearing, friendship networks, and access to socioeconomic resources. Culturally, the infant benefits from beliefs and values defining children as desirable and attractive, as well as those specifying that children should be cared for and not be abused. For the parents, culture provides guidance as to how the infant should be reared and usually provides moral support for undertaking the child-rearing function.

Obstacles.   For the infant, obstacles are those factors which impede growth and development. Given the infant's fragility, obstacles can easily be life-threatening. For the parents, efforts to care for the infant can be blocked through a variety of obstacles. Biologically, the infant's genetic equipment may be incomplete or partially nonfunctional, making it more difficult for him or her to perform life-sustaining activities or interact with the environment so that growth and development occur. This would be the case for infants born without an organ or a limb; with a defective organ, such as the heart; or with brain damage. An infant who contracted a disease would also be placed at a risk. An unusual or undesirable physical appearance can also be an obstacle, for example a hair lip, cross-eyes, or a limb deformity. Parents may also encounter biological obstacles. The blind or deaf parent, for instance, has a much more difficult job relating to the child in order to perceive and meet its needs.

For the child, psychological obstacles relate closely to its biological capacity to perceive and organize the environment and to process information cognitively. The development of fearful or rigid personality responses to stimuli may also be an obstacle to continued growth. These chronic distress responses can also precipitate unhelpful behaviors by others. Parents' personality patterns can be obstacles when they lead to compulsive activities toward the infant which restrict rather than enhance its growth. Social-structural obstacles for the child revolve around inadequate nutrition, physical care, and nurturance that may result from poverty, family structures that cannot sustain child-rearing activities, disorganized communities, and parents who have not had the opportunity to learn how to parent. These factors also operate as obstacles for parents. Cultural obstacles include beliefs and values that denigrate certain types of infants, such as the deformed, the illegitimate, the "fussy," and those of minority races and ethnic groups. Culture can also be an obstacle when it mandates child care practices that conflict with biological needs, for example excessively early toilet training or ancient Chinese feet-binding practices. For parents who are members of certain groups, cultural values and beliefs that preach that they cannot or should not rear children are obstacles. In the United States, this applies to single parents, homosexuals, and the physically handicapped, among others. Members of these groups can and do successfully care for infants, but they have to fight dominant cultural values and beliefs representing them as incompetent.

Implications for Social Work. Infants need a great deal of care if they are to thrive and develop. This requires many resources, including knowledge, money, energy, love, food, shelter, and time. Many parents may lack these resources, and the support systems available to them may be similarly depleted. The social worker needs to be able to assess the resources available, always taking into account the child-rearing strategies appropriate to a person's cultural environment.

The infant may also need help. A child born with a genetic limitation or who suffers a severe illness needs careful diagnostic and treatment resources. Parents and others may need financial help to pay for these services, as well as knowledge and emotional support to be able to use them most effectively. An infant needing special care often imposes substantial strains on the whole family system, and the resulting needs have to be addressed by the social worker. Relationships between the infant and the parents can also be affected.

In the American myth, the infant is enshrined in a cradle of affluence and acceptance. However, this myth does not always agree with reality. Babies are sometimes burdens on already strained financial, emotional, or time resources. When they require special care they can be even more disruptive. Understanding the joys as well as the heartaches of infancy as a life stage for infants and parents alike requires the social worker's careful analysis and sensitivity.

Middle and Late Childhood as a Life Stage

Tasks.   Middle and late childhood in this book is defined as the period from approximately ages four to twelve. It is a period during which biological development continues to be very important but comes to be shaped more and more by social interaction in an increasingly wide range of social situations. Childhood tasks are to continue the biological growth and development necessary for healthy organic functioning as well as to lay the foundation for lifelong personality characteristics and cognitive functioning. Physical health, personality strength and adaptability, and cognitive capacity form the foundation for lifelong participation as a member of society. The tasks of childhood, then, serve individual growth needs as well as society's efforts to socialize people to become supporters of the social system. As children become more self-sufficient, their impact on parental roles is lessened. In addition, by this time the parents have usually adjusted to their children's needs. Therefore, the focus in this section will be on children exclusively rather than both children and parents.

Resources.   Biological resources available to children are similar to those available to infants so they need not be discussed further here. Sometimes, though, it is only when a child begins school and interacts with a wider range of people than those in his or her family that particular biological resources are noted. This could include unusually developed coordination, muscle strength, hearing and eyesight, and overall resistance to disease. Psychological resources also continue to develop from infancy, but they are especially important in childhood. Substantial cognitive development occurs in school and through the behavior models of peers, family members, and media personalities. The child endowed genetically with high intelligence, sound perceptual organs, and general health enabling these genetic endowments to be fully developed has important biological/psychological resources for his or her use in confronting childhood tasks. Psychological development, including the development of intelligence, is also strongly related to social experiences, as will be discussed further below. Continued physical and social stimulation that confronts children with challenging but manage-able stresses helps them develop a sense of competence and well-being. Continued parental nurturance and support also facilitate the development of a stable self-identity which can adapt to increasing-ly diversified and new life experiences.

Social-structural resources continue to be important to a per-son's development from infancy through childhood. Family struc-ture, community environment, school systems, and friendship net-works are extremely important sources of opportunities for the child to encounter new people and situations. When these structures sup-port the child's biological growth and psychological development they become extremely powerful resources. For example, parents who are supportive of exploratory activities by the child and who gently cushion occasional failures help make the world seem a rich and exciting place. Schools that stimulate cognitive and social de-velopment by presenting manageable challenges in a structured but supportive context also encourage a sense of security through growth. Cultural values can be resources when they mandate re-spect for children's needs and involvement of children in the full range of life activities. For example, children who know their grand-parents are exposed to cross-generational learning that they might otherwise miss, and children who participate in appropriate adult activities, or activities culturally defined as such, are better prepared to perform them when they are adults themselves.

Obstacles. Biological obstacles in infancy often become in-creasingly limiting as the child grows and is exposed to increased demands. The malnourished child may find it difficult to play with friends or to concentrate in school. The child with limited physical mobility may become increasingly isolated from his or her active peers. Sometimes biological obstacles only become apparent in childhood. Hearing or vision loss are common examples of deficits that are commonly discovered in school. Biological obstacles be-come increasingly enmeshed in a web of relationships with social structures, and their ultimate significance in a child's life will de-pend on how these relationships are developed. The child with cere-bral palsy who is seen as an embarrassment will not receive needed therapy and will gradually become weaker and less mobile. The child with an uncorrected vision deficit will find school a frustrating, boring experience and may act out as a result. Even a child who has to wear glasses may be ridiculed by his or her peers and gradually withdraw socially. Mitigating these effects of obstacles requires careful medical diagnosis and supportive social relationships.

Psychological obstacles are frequently tied to biological ones — although they also reflect social obstacles, as we will see. The child with cognitive limitations or perceptual deficits may find demands by others difficult to understand and impossible to fulfill. Even psychological and biological resources can be overwhelmed by excessive or harsh demands that generate fear, anxiety, withdrawal, and rigidity. Whenever the world is seen as cruel, unmanageable, and threatening the child's psychological development is likely to be restricted so that it lessens the ability to understand and adapt flexibly and productively to situations. The reasons the environment seems so hostile may have biological, social, or cultural roots, but the results are similar regardless of their sources. Therefore, we can expect that a child of average intelligence who is regularly pushed into educational and social situations beyond his or her abilities will react with hostility, anxiety, and withdrawal. Of course the amount of interpersonal support the child receives will influence the kind of personality that ultimately develops.

Social-structural obstacles can be many for the child. Any structured social events that reduce the child's sense of safety, security, competence, mastery, or health become obstacles. Such events can be caused by poverty (chronic ill health, hunger, anxiety over physical safety), racism or other forms of prejudice and discrimination (physical attacks, attacks on one's identity and personal integrity), natural disasters, accidents, unhealthy family structures (child abuse, either physical or mental), unhealthy school structures (rigid, overly demanding, non-supportive situations), and even peer groups that scapegoat a child. Since the child moves increasingly into a broader range of social situations, its contact with social-structural resources and obstacles is greatly increased over that of the infant. Cultural obstacles are those values and beliefs that inhibit the child's development. Excessive protectiveness can be as great a cultural obstacle as beliefs that ignore the child's need for privacy, play, protection, and nurturing.

Implications for Social Work.   Childhood is the critical beginning of a person's interactions with a complex environment. These interactions are an important part of growth, but they can easily become overwhelming and restricting. For some children, the environment may be too unstructured or too lacking in interaction opportunities to provide the challenges necessary for growth. For others, the environment may be too structured and demanding. Social workers need to be able to assess the ways in which existing environments are able to respond to a child's efforts to understand, adapt, and grow. Sometimes environments need to be enriched, other times they need to be simplified. In all cases, the focus is on helping the child find the resources needed in a particular environment — whether those resources be family activities, available life-sustaining resources, school system activities, or something else.

There is considerable agreement among theories that childhood is a time when the basic personality is established. While it is subject to modification throughout life, a view of the world as essentially benign or fearsome seems to be established by the end of childhood. At this life stage, then, the interaction between the individual and the environment is especially critical. Adults frequently have enough knowledge and power to modify the child's environment if they feel the need to do so, but the child has relatively little power to do this. Thus it is the job of social work efforts to focus on making the environment as supportive as possible for the child's efforts to grow and develop both biologically and socially.

Adolescence as a Life Stage

Tasks.   The major tasks of adolescence, defined here as approximately ages thirteen to eighteen, revolve around biological development and further integration into social institutions. Adolescence is characterized by somewhat selective biological developments. Basic motor, perceptual, and cognitive maturation has already occurred in infancy and childhood. In adolescence there is generally a substantial increase in physical size, height, and weight. Sexual maturation also occurs, including the emergence of secondary sex characteristics, such as breast development, body hair, and so on. The rapid size growth and sexual maturation that occur involve substantial hormonal changes that can affect physical appearance and emotional needs. A large part of the adolescent's task, then, is to adjust to changes in body image, physical capacities, and sexual needs.

These biological changes take place within a social context that is also changing. School demands are more academically rigorous and are increasingly related to lifelong planning. For example, academic success affects college choice and in turn career opportunities. School also becomes an increasingly important social arena in which peer group pressure accelerates. Lifelong friendships and interaction patterns can be established at this time. Biological development, academic demands, and peer pressure naturally intersect. The adolescent confronts a changing self, making it difficult to understand precisely what his or her needs and capabilities are. The friendship patterns that characterized childhood may suddenly seem inappropriate as young people struggle to find acceptance among their peers. Intellectual capacity, physical skill, and physical appearance are dimensions that heavily influence the kinds of social demands and opportunities available to an adolescent. This is further affected by the child's race, ethnicity, and sex. For example, a young woman who matures and grows in size early in her adolescence may feel awkward and sexually vulnerable, while one who experiences these events later may be better ready to integrate them into her social relationships with others. The reverse is true for young men, who tend to grow and mature later than women. But the young man whose development is late even for his sex often comes to feel weak and unattractive.

Naturally the support adolescents get from others is critical to their development. This can be problematic for parents who experience anxiety over the increasing size, competence, demands, and autonomy of their children. Rather than assisting their children's development, they may try to maintain their parental control by denying the adolescent's new-found competence or by emphasizing the significance of biological changes in order to increase the young person's sense of uncertainty and hence his or her need for parental protection. Other adults, especially teachers, can also reinforce either the youngster's sense of developing strength and well-being or his or her awkwardness and anxiety. From society's point of view adolescence is a time of some normative flexibility so that biological changes and the erratic approaches to need-meeting they sometimes create can be accommodated. Yet society still expects that by the end of adolescence the developing adult will be ready to assume a relatively stable niche as an adult in the social order.

Resources.   As suggested above, the adolescent's physical resources are often prodigious. Physical strength and size are powerful resources, as are the continued strengthening of perceptual and cognitive abilities. Adequate nutrition is an important resource during this period. Sexual functioning matures during adolescence — itself a powerful motivator for behavior. Psychologically, adolescents bring their biological abilities to bear on establishing enduring patterns of relationships with their peers and with adults. These become important beginnings of support systems that will continue throughout life. Perceptual and cognitive resources are especially important for meeting increasing societal demands for achievement in an expanding range of areas — among which school, work, and family are especially important. Through this process, the personality is gradually enriched by increasing mutuality in relationships, deepening of interests, and a clearer articulation of personal values and goals.

Social-structural resources are those which promote the adolescent's sense of competence and need for individuation. The family continues to be an important potential source of support, and the peer group assumes increased importance as an influence on behavior. School becomes a potential source of enrichment, while the youngster's increased size and physical and mental capacities enable him or her to participate in a wider range of institutional activities, such as driving, working, church-related groups, school-sponsored trips and activities, and so on. Culturally, values become very importance resources, helping adolescents solidify their self-identity and self-image as well as order personal values and lifelong priorities. Decisions about the balance between work and family, self and others, achievement and sharing, and stability and change grow out of cultural values.

Obstacles. Biological development can be an obstacle in a variety of ways during adolescence. The biological changes that occur may not be well understood and may therefore create social difficulties. The young person's body development is a case in point. Changes in size and strength can create appearance and behavior characteristics that are denigrated by others — the very tall young woman or the overly enthusiastic but slightly uncontrolled and uncoordinated young man, are two instances of adolescents who receive such treatment. Illness and accidents are also possible when physical growth is not supported by adequate nutrition or when growth between the various parts of the body is not synchronous. Hormonal changes are common and can create farily rapid and extensive fluctuations in energy levels, moods, and sense of well being. Physical and psychological changes are closely related, since for the adolescent the emerging adult body is a critical component of self-image and treatment by others. Developmental irregularities or problems often bring ridicule and isolation during adolescence, which in turn can have powerful effects on feelings of competence and well-being. This is especially true if childhood experiences had begun the process of accentuating weaknesses rather than strengths. However, perceptual and cognitive capacities can be used to mitigate the negative psychological effects of physical obstacles. The very intelligent woman, for example, may be treated with respect even though she may not be pretty by conventional definitions.

Social-structural obstacles limit development by restricting access to resources or creating social expectations that are inhibiting. Poor adolescents may lack proper nutrition or may need medical care to deal with myopia (near-sightedness), a biological condition which often accompanies the rapid growth of adolescence. Families may have unrealistic social or academic expectations for their children and thus push them into situations in which success is practically impossible. Schools sometimes emphasize young people's weaknesses, which may then create or reinforce peer group difficulties. The peer group itself can be an extremely damaging obstacle as it forces young people to conform to stereotyped expectations regarding dress, behavior, and interpersonal relationships. Cultural values can further exacerbate social-structural obstacles by legitimating disadvantaging expectations. For instance, bright women are hurt by cultural values that restrict women to the home, and physically limited men are denigrated by values that emphasize large physical size and strength. Since socialization is such an important part of the adolescent's developing and maturing sense of self, cultural values can greatly shape — and inhibit — personal growth and development.

Implications for Social Work. During any type of change, either personal or social, people are put at a risk. Therefore their efforts to understand and find appropriate responses to changes need to be strongly supported. Otherwise the uncertainties accompanying change can gradually erode one's sense of competence. Supporting people through change entails providing information, emotional resources, and help in keeping the pieces of shifting institutional relationships in balance. For example, social workers often help adolescents manage relationships between their emerging sexuality, their desire for rewarding interpersonal relationships, increasing autonomy at home, and school demands. In doing this, of course, many people have to be involved besides the adolescent himself or herself.

Social workers are also heavily involved with modifying social expectations for adolescents. Although there is some flexibility built into the role of adolescent, there are many inconsistencies and strains in role definitions. For example, men are generally allowed to be more sexually promiscuous than are women. Therefore, some groups of adolescents — here, females — may be punished for behavior permissible for others. Social workers attempt to make social expectations more equitable, and when adolescents are punished, to protect their needs for support and care — preventing their acquiring prison records if possible, keeping them from being expelled from school, avoiding unnecessary estrangement from their families, and so on. Often the family is a major source of difficulty in the development of appropriate perceptions of and responses to the needs of adolescents, explaining in part why social workers so often work with families. Adolescents can sometimes appear gawky, homely, and unloveable as they struggle to understand their own bodies and function effectively in the world around them. Social workers try to help the individual adolescent and society — his or her family, teachers, peers, and so on — approach each other with greater awareness, caring, and support.

Adulthood as a Life Stage

Task. Adulthood can be divided into three major periods: young adulthood, roughly from eighteen to twenty-five years of age; middle adulthood, roughly from twenty-five to forty-five; and late adulthood, roughly from forty-five to sixty-one. Although each period has somewhat distinctive tasks, resources, and obstacles, for the purposes of this book we can talk about adulthood as a whole. Readers are encouraged to think and study on their own about the three subparts. Adulthood is a time of accomplishment and productivity — probably the period when most people are the most goal-directed with respect to their own life aspirations. However, society expects that individual aspirations will mesh with societal needs. For example, rearing children requires resources that are earned — and spent — through the economic system. Socialization in childhood and adolescence is the major mechanism through which adults are prepared to work toward their life goals in socially acceptable ways. Individual goals and societal goals, then, are assumed to come together during adulthood. At no other life stage is the individual quite so oriented toward the performance of societal tasks. Naturally members of diverse groups process societal goals and means of achieving them through their own particular values, resources, and obstacles.

In addition to working toward the attainment of task goals, adulthood is a time when one seeks interpersonal intimacy. Enduring relationships with others are formed, some of which generally include sexual activity. Marriage is, of course, one pattern, but others include parenting relationships, non-married coupling, and selected friendships. The adult's sense of accomplishment and well-being are for most people heavily dependent on the formation of close interpersonal relationships that provide important social, biological, and psychological supports. While adulthood is a period of autonomous goal-seeking behavior carried out in the major institutions of society, it is also a time of personal nurturance through the special relationships found in adulthood — marriage or other forms of coupling, parenting, and so on. Thus, in a sense adulthood is both outward and inward focused, a time of both independence and interdependence.

Resources.   In adulthood people usually have as many physical resources as they will ever have. Although physical development continues, gradually moving into increasingly degenerative conditions, adulthood is generally characterized by well-developed physical, perceptual, cognitive, and psychological resources. Levels of development vary, of course, but cannot be substantially changed in adulthood. Their use can vary, however. Use is a function of social-structural variables which either facilitates or inhibits adult behavior.

Social-structural resources for adults are found primarily in the major institutions of society which serve to organize people's behavior around the performance of significant life tasks. Through the family and family-like structures, adults solidify their most intimate interpersonal relationships. The economic institution, that is, the combination of enterprises that make up the economy, is generally the arena in which men achieve their task-oriented goals. This is also increasingly true for women, although women have also traditionally achieved many task goals through the family, in the form of child-rearing. The political institution interacts extensively with the economic institution and also provides opportunities for significant decision making. The educational, religious, and social welfare institutions are also often supportive of task as well as interpersonal behaviors. Inevitably, the interactions between adults and social institutions vary for different types of adults. While the institutional structure is intended to support the goal-directed behavior of Anglo-Saxon males, we saw in an earlier chapter that it may affect other adults quite differently. Cultural values support adults' efforts to be independent in most of their interpersonal behaviors. However, we will see below that independence is not always functional and that dominant cultural values in the United States tend to arbitrarily limit the range of socially acceptable interpersonal behaviors.

Obstacles. While illness and accidents can occur at any point in the life cycle, higher rates of both begin to characterize middle and late adulthood. This reflects the stress that accompanies adult life tasks as well as the range of behaviors in which adults engage. For example, work-related accidents and illnesses occur primarily in adulthood, since it spans the major working years. Also, a great deal of violence occurs in the context of the family, especially between adults. Even the biological life process begins very gradually to shift toward degenerative processes, so that there begins to be a lessening of vision, hearing, strength, and quickness of cognitive processes. These changes are not usually substantial enough to have a major effect on behavior during adulthood, but their influence does grow cumulatively.

A major potential obstacle in adulthood is the gradual deterioration of personality adaptiveness. This may result in part from physical changes that are perceived as modifying appearance and behavior in undesirable ways. Even such relatively unimportant biological changes as the loss or graying of hair or changes in skin texture can generate anxiety and defensiveness. Adults sometimes deny these physical changes by using cosmetics, wearing different clothes, or even associating with younger, more "attractive," people. This can have seriously disruptive consequences for long-established and important supportive relationships with spouses, mates, siblings, close friends, and others. The loss of these supports can undermine the individual's personality resources and may lead to depression or other types of alienation and isolation.

A second assault on psychological functioning in adulthood results from the interplay of social-structural and personality variables. Adulthood is, as has been noted, the principal period in the life cycle when cherished life goals are sought through such activities as work, peer relationships, family or family-like relationships, and so on. However, it is only in rare cases that all of these goals are attained, and during adulthood the individual has to begin to come to terms with this reality. Social-structural resources naturally play a significant role in an individual's ability to achieve life goals. Poverty, destructive family or family-like relationships, unemployment, accidents or injuries, and the loss of loved ones can all block goal attainment. When this occurs, the individual's own sense of identity and self-worth are called into question. Even worse, there seems less and less time left in life to try again. One's sense of personal and societal failure is further exacerbated by dominant cultural values stressing success — especially financial success — and achievement. Psychological responses can include a whole range of defensive actions sometimes even as extreme as changing the place in which one lives so that the failure will not be so apparent. Cultural values may also inhibit the efforts of diverse groups to meet the needs of their adult members. For example, homosexuals may be pressured into loveless heterosexual marriages and furtive homosexual contacts, and many women may accept physical and emotional abuse rather than endure the stigma of divorce — even today when divorce is much more common than in the past.

Implications for Social Work. Adulthood is a long and complex life stage, encompassing the period in life when firm life commitments are made to people and tasks. These, of course, are modified and renegotiated as time goes on and as people adjust to the changing relationship between their goals and accomplishments. This may, for example, include divorce and remarriage (or similar events for non-married couples) and job or career changes. Energy also changes, so that motivation that may have been keen in earlier stages of adulthood may gradually disappear. Yet, if there is such a phenomenon as overall satisfaction with one's life, its roots are in adulthood — the time of life when goals are formulated and when the most significant efforts are made to achieve them. If these goals are substantially achieved, life is usually seen as happy; if not, the future may look bleak indeed.

Obviously adulthood is a time of excitement, challenge, and stress. Social workers need to be prepared to support people in their efforts and to help them cope with such stresses of adult life as work pressure, relationship problems, and parenting demands. It is also critical that the social structure reward people's plans and activities. Institutionalized discrimination, for instance, systematically blocks the efforts of certain groups to achieve their goals. In offering help, social workers need to recognize that adults are a very special group with which to work. They often strongly value their independence and autonomy, as cultural values have taught them to, and not infrequently resist offers of help by others, even professionals. A sense of competence is extremely important for adults, and social workers have to exercise the utmost care in supporting and preserving it. At the same time, adulthood is a time of stress and challenge during which personal support and institutional intervention are frequently needed.

Retirement as a Life Stage

Tasks. Retirement, defined in this book as the period from approximately age sixty-two to death, is a period of adjustment to loss. It is a time when biological capacities continue to degenerate, when many productive roles — especially the roles of work and parenting — are left behind, and when significant others in one's life are lost through death. Retirement also involves planning for reduced earning capacity, changed living arrangements, and increased health care needs. And as importantly as any other life task, retirement entails preparing for death. Obviously this life stage is one of tremendous change and adjustment, both biologically and socially. Indeed, these two areas interact closely, and the nature of their interaction is the major determinant of whether retirement is a time of contentment or desperation. On the other hand, retirement is also a time of freedom from many of the tasks of earlier life stages, such as work, interpersonal responsibilities, and child-rearing. This allows more opportunity to engage in quiet contemplation and personally rewarding activities than is usually possible when one is younger and under more pressure.

Resources. While old age entails unavoidable physical deterioration in a number of areas, most older people continue to have relatively good health and retain most of their earlier perceptual and cognitive capacities until very advanced old age. Of course, people age differently just as they differ in so many other ways, and some people experience advanced physical deterioration at relatively young ages. Nevertheless, most people are able to carry on their usual physical activities during retirement with relatively minor adjustments. Physical energy is used differently, however. Older people tend to avoid the hectic pace younger people prefer and think their actions through more carefully before initiating them. In this sense, the elderly become more efficient, reflecting once again the strong tie between physical and psychological resources. Looking back on a lifetime of accomplishments, most older people find self-validation and satisfaction, so they can adjust to lower energy levels by focusing on what is meaningful to them rather than primarily on what society expects.

The relatively recent organization of retired people into vocal pressure groups has helped strengthen social-structural resources for the elderly. A variety of financial aid programs exist to help maintain income in old age, as well as other concrete support services such as housing and transportation subsidies, in-home meal programs, and medical care services. More of these services are needed, however, especially for some groups of elderly persons. Additional social needs are increasingly being recognized and met through self-help groups, the development of recreational programs, the creation of educational opportunities, and the provision of personal counseling services. There is a special emphasis now on structuring institutional arrangements so that older people can retain control over their own lives. Some of these arrangements currently being developed are housing that builds in both autonomy and immediate access to help, transportation systems that are more physically and financially accessible to the elderly, and counseling and financial supports to help link the older person to some type of family or family-like network. There is little doubt that existing social-structural arrangements impinge on the quality of life of older persons as they do on groups at other life cycle stages.

Cultural values have become extremely important determinants of the nature of retirement, and once again self-help groups organized among older persons have had a noticeable impact. When the extended family is a common social-structural form, older people are usually taken care of primarily within the family unit. This is much less common in the nuclear family. However, other values also affect the treatment of the elderly. In a society that values autonomy and productivity the elderly may not want to be limited by the roles they are relegated to within the family. They may prefer to be socially and sexually active even if the primary spouse or mate dies, leading to the formation of new families and family-like units among older persons. They may also wish to define for themselves the extent of their involvement with children, grandchildren, and the economic system, rather than automatically assuming roles expected of them within their initial families of procreation. All of these structural changes reflect cultural values that are gradually changing to accommodate a much greater degree of independence and variation in the behavior of the elderly.

Obstacles. Even for the relatively healthy older person, increasing old age brings greater risks of illness, accidents, and physical deterioration. This progressively limits the person's physical mobility and social participation. It may also strain the financial resources available to the older person. Gradually, the individual becomes more dependent on others. This can threaten his or her sense of self-identity and well-being. Combined with a commonly experienced gradual loss of perceptual acuity — especially sight, hearing, and taste — the older person may withdraw and become increasingly isolated. This often reduces his or her motivation for living, which can manifest itself in reduced food intake to the point of malnutrition and a lack of mobility and stimulation that accelerate physical deterioration.

While there has been greatly increased recognition of the needs of the elderly in recent decades, social-structural factors still make retirement problematic. Young people grow up detached from older people so they don't learn how to prepare for this life stage. The abrupt loss of social roles that occurs when grown children move out of the home, sometimes called the "empty nest" syndrome, and when the worker has to retire, leave people feeling useless and undirected. The high cost of medical care creates anxieties that old age will lead to destitution. These conditions are perpetuated by cultural values that overemphasize youth and physical appearance, as well as productivity and independence. United States society values progress and change and is always pushing toward the new with little respect for its own past or those who created it. In such a milieu, it is little wonder that older people feel left behind and left out. We know only too well that these feelings are closely tied to accelerated biological deterioration, social isolation, psychological distress, and self-destruction. Unfortunately, these are realities for many of the elderly.

Implications for Social Work. Like any type of diversity, old age has its particular resources and obstacles. Society holds conflicting views about the elderly. On one hand it assumes that older people are physical and emotional cripples, and on the other hand it tries to find ways to make them more self-sufficient, since they make up a growing percentage of the population. Social workers, as part of their commitment to help people live contented, self-directed lives, must reinforce societal efforts to recognize and support the many strengths of older people. For example, there is a need for many more apartment complexes that allow the elderly to live autonomously and still have access to immediate physical help and social companionship. There is also a need for nursing homes in which the older person's right to and need for privacy — including the privacy to express their sexuality — is respected. Many other services are needed as well.

At the interpersonal level, social workers must be sensitive to older people's continuing need for friendship, social recognition, and intimate ties to others. An older person may need emotional support to adjust to a radically altered physical appearance or decreased physical mobility. A strong sense of self-respect is as important in retirement as it is at any other point in the life cycle. Help in meeting daily living needs is also sometimes of critical importance. This could include help in such diverse activities as securing transportation to the doctor, applying for financial assistance, or selecting a nursing home. For the older person, most of the life cycle is over. Much of the social worker's task may be to help the individual reflect back on the past, putting pieces together so that the wholeness and richness of the mosaic becomes apparent. This sense of accomplishment is an important part of the individual's source of strength when preparing for the next — and last — life stage.

Death as a Life Stage

Throughout this chapter we have been trying to present a framework useable for analyzing human behavior in its social context at any point in the life cycle. The first part of the chapter described the framework itself. This was followed by the use of the framework to analyze the following life stages: conception and birth, infancy, childhood, adolescence, adulthood, and retirement. Now we would like to give you the opportunity to use the framework yourself to analyze death as a life stage. Hopefully this will increase your mastery of it as well as your sense of confidence in its use. To assist you, we have provided some general guidelines below.

Before moving to the analytical framework, it will probably be helpful to stop and think for a minute about your own attitudes towards death. Young people are frequently shielded from death as a part of life: hospitals usually do not allow them to visit patients until they are adolescents, they are not taken to funerals, and they have very little contact with the elderly. When something is unfamiliar it often seems strange and even frightening. Many readers may feel this way about death. Yet today there is a rich literature about death and dying that can help one understand better this part of the life cycle (see this chapter's bibliography for specific titles). As a social worker, you will need to feel professionally comfortable practicing in situations that include death or dying — when doing hospital social work, for example. We have already seen that human life and social structures are characterized by diversity — a fact that social workers must learn to understand and appreciate. Death and dying is another element of this diversity. As you use the framework to analyze death as part of the life cycle, remind yourself that it is as important, as complex, and as fascinating as any other life cycle stage. Also understand that you will need to understand and deal with death and dying as a social work professional regardless of your personal feelings about their part in your own life.

Tasks. Think about the life tasks with which the individual and society are faced at death. What do each gain and what do each lose? One way to help you think this through is to try to imagine what would happen if people lived forever. What problems would be created that death helps solve? Another thing to think about is why people fear death — what they are really afraid of, and how understanding their fear helps one understand the life tasks to be accomplished at death. And, by the way, does thinking about death in terms of life tasks make it easier or more difficult for you to think about your own death?

Resources. Using the biological/psychological/social-structural/cultural format, determine what resources people have as they try to carry out the life tasks associated with death. Another way to think about this is in terms of those factors that make it easier for people to die. These might be biological factors, such as drugs; psychological factors, such as emotional security; social-structural factors, such as legal procedures to pass on resources to others; and cultural factors, such as beliefs about an afterlife and rituals to help people prepare for death. Resources, then, are the things that support people's efforts to die in such a way as to maximize their sense of personal and social well-being. Does it seem a contradiction to think of well-being at the point of death? Why or why not?

Obstacles. The opposite side of the resource coin would be the biological/psychological/social-structural/cultural factors that make it more difficult for people to die. Think about pain, for example. Is it a resource, making it easier to die, or an obstacle, making it harder, or both? In thinking about obstacles, be sure to include relationships with others. When do relationships make it more difficult to die? When do they make it easier? Do you have difficulty thinking about obstacles, especially in relation to death? Why is this a painful subject for you, or why isn't it?

Implications for Social Work. What aspects of dying should social workers be especially sensitive to? Remember to think systematically so that you do not overlook help that those associated with the dying person might need, as well as help for the dying person himself or herself. As you think about it, are there resources the social worker might need in order to work effectively in the highly emotional situations in which death often occurs? What might these be, and would they include structural supports as well as personal resources? Could *you* work with someone in the last life cycle stage? Think carefully about the problems you would anticipate if such a situation were part of your work responsibilities. How does such thinking help you understand the implications of death as a life stage for the social work profession?

Conclusion

The life cycle is a concept that helps social workers analyze human behavior in order to better understand the service needs that can be anticipated throughout life. The analytical framework used is one that relates directly to the discussion of systems and human diversity in earlier chapters. Looking at life stages in terms of life tasks and the interplay of resources and obstacles in people's efforts to perform them is consistent with the focus in chapter 5 on goal-directed behavior.

It is apparent that the life cycle encompasses a relentless progression of changes: some from within the organism itself and others generated by the external human and physical environment. Yet amid these changes there are some constants. These include certain lifelong tasks, namely, physical survival, physical development within the limits set by one's genetic inheritance, attempts to relate to others, developing and strengthening a sense of self-worth and competence, and task-focused behavior. We have seen how these constants are shaped somewhat differently at each life stage, and how the basic tasks remain constant nevertheless. Each life stage then adds its own particular tasks. Using the life cycle to understand behavior thus leads us back to two important points made much earlier in this book. One is that human behavior involves the interaction between people and their environments. The second is that human beings have common human needs that are elaborated and met in extraordinarily diverse ways. The next and last chapter will examine further some implications of these two points.

Study Questions

1. Use the framework presented in figure 5.2 to analyze yourself at the life stage in which you now are. First, of course, identity the life stage and explain why you feel it is your current life cycle stage. After doing your own analysis, go back to the chapter's discussion of your life stage. Based on your analysis, do you feel the chapter has omitted, overemphasized, or under-emphasized any aspect of the life stage? Discuss what you feel should be added or subtracted and why.

2. Now do the same type of analysis for someone you know well who is in a different life stage. A grandparent or younger sibling would be possible choices. Be sure to identify the life stage, analyze it, and compare your analysis with the discussion in the text. Which analysis did you find easier — this one or the analysis of your own life cycle stage? Why?

3. Think back to what you have learned about the life cycle in other courses — psychology, human development, sociology, and so forth. In what ways is the knowledge presented in this chapter similar and in what ways different? Do the approaches interrelate and support each other? Why or why not? Is one more appealing to you than the others? In what ways?

4. Choose one life stage and one ethnic group, such as a Euro-American group, an Hispanic group, an Asian-American group, or a Native American group. For the life stage you have selected, analyze in detail the resources and obstacles the group you have chosen faces at that life stage. After your analysis is complete, summarize your view of the ease with which members of that group are likely to perform the tasks of the life stage selected for study.

5. Which life stage interests you most? What about it interests you? How important have your own personal experiences been in creating this interest? Perform a similar analysis for the life cycle stage that interests you least. Do you find that your interests have led to your having much more information about the preferred life stage? Why or why not?

Additional Readings on the Life Cycle

There is a voluminous amount of literature pertinent to the life cycle. It includes works attempting to develop theories of human development through the life cycle, presentations of data about the life cycle experiences, and efforts to bring together theory and data into an integrated view of the life cycle. This is a very selective bibliography that emphasizes the integrative task, but it is sufficient for those who wish to explore any other aspect of the life cycle literature.

Atchley, Robert. *The Social Forces in Later Life*. Belmont, Ca.: Wadsworth Press, 1972.

Brody, Elaine. "Aging." In *The Encyclopedia of Social Work*. 17th ed. Washington, D.C.: National Association of Social Workers, 1977.

Eisdorfer, Carl and Lawton, M. Powell eds. *The Psychology of Adult Development and Aging*. Washington, D.C.: American Psychological Association, 1973.

Erikson, Erik. *Childhood and Society*. 2nd ed. New York: Norton, 1964.

Erikson, Erik. *Identity, Youth and Crisis*. New York: Norton, 1968.

Ganter, Grace and Yeakel, Margaret. *Human Behavior in the Social Environment*. New York: Columbia University Press, 1980.

Gould, Roger. *Transformations: Growth and Change in Adult Life*. New York: Simon and Shuster, 1978.

Havighurst, Robert. *Developmental Tasks and Education*. 3rd ed. New York: David McKay Co., 1972.

Kalish, Richard. *Late Adulthood: Perspectives on Human Development*. Monterey, Ca.: Brooks/Cole, 1975.

Kubler-Ross, Elizabeth. *Death: The Final Stage of Growth*. Englewood Cliffs, N. J.: Prentice-Hall, 1971.

———, *On Death and Dying*. New York: Macmillan, 1971.

Langer, Jonas. *Theories of Development.* New York: Holt, Rinehart, and Winston, 1969.

Lidz, Theodore. *The Person: His and Her Development Throughout the Life Cycle.* Rev. 2nd ed. New York: Basic Books, 1976.

Lugo, James O. and Hershey, Gerald. *Human Development: A Psychological, Biological, and Sociological Approach to the Life Span.* 2nd ed. New York: Macmillan, 1979.

Munro, Robert and Munro, Ruth. *Cross-Cultural Human Development.* Monterey, Ca.: Brooks/Cole, 1975.

Troll, Lillian. *Early and Middle Adulthood.* Monterey, Ca.: Brooks/Cole, 1975.

Additional Readings on Aging and Death

Butler, Robert N. *Why Survive: Being Old in America.* New York: Harper & Row, 1975.

Butler, Robert N. and Lewis, Myrna I. *Aging and Mental Health: Positive Psychological Approaches.* 2nd ed. St. Louis: C. V. Mosby, 1977.

Carse, James P. and Dallery, Arlene B., eds. *Death and Society: A Book of Readings and Sources.* New York: Harcourt, Brace, Jovanovich, 1977.

Cristofer, Michael. *The Shadow Box.* New York: Drama Book Specialists, 1977.

Curtis, Sharon R. *Nobody Ever Died of Old Age.* Boston: Little, Brown, 1972.

Halamandaris, Val J. *Too Old, Too Sick, Too Bad.* Germantown, Md.: Aspen Systems Corporation, 1977.

Harbert, Anita S. and Ginsberg, Leon H. *Human Services for Older Adults: Concepts and Skills.* Belmont, Ca.: Wadsworth Publishing, 1979.

Hendin, D. *Death as a Fact of Life.* New York: Norton, 1973.

Kalish, Richard A. *Death, Grief and Caring.* Monterey, Ca.: Brooks/Cole, 1980.

Kastenbaum, Robert J. *Death, Society, and the Human Experience.* St. Louis: C. V. Mosby, 1977.

Lowy, Louis. *Social Work with the Aging.* New York: Harper & Row, 1979.

Marks, Elaine and de Beauvoir, Simone. *Encounters with Death.* New Brunswick, N. J.: Rutgers University Press, 1973.

Marshall, Victor W. *Last Chapters: A Sociology of Aging and Dying.* Monterey, Ca.: Brooks/Cole, 1980.

Orcott, Ben A., et al., eds. *Social Work and Thanatology.* New York: Arno, 1980.

National Council on Aging. *Fact Book on Aging: A Profile of America's Older Population.* Washington, D.C.: National Council on Aging, 1978.

Prichard, Elizabeth R. and Collard, Jean, eds. *Social Work with the Dying Patient and His Family*. New York: Columbia University Press, 1977.

Schneidman, Edwin S., ed. *Death: Current Perspectives*. Palo Alto, Ca.: Mayfield Publishing, 1976.

Simos, Bertha G. *A Time to Grieve: Loss as a Universal Human Experience*. New York: Family Service Association of America, 1979.

Epilogue

The professional purposes of social work serve as guidelines for practice. They also provide the focus for professional education, since what is learned should help practitioners achieve the purposes of the profession. Throughout this book we have tried to emphasize the links between knowledge, analysis, and action. It is impossible to make informed professional decisions about what to *do* unless a social worker has the knowledge needed to analyze the practice situation he or she confronts. This book has focused on knowledge that is likely to be most helpful to social workers and has sought to show how a wide range of specific concepts can be integrated and applied to practice situations.

In carrying out its goal, this book has emphasized three perspectives for viewing human behavior: systems, human diversity, and goal-directed behavior. Now that these perspectives are familiar to the reader they can be looked at in ways that go beyond the scope of this book. Let's take each in turn.

Systems. The systems perspective helps the social worker see the range of interrelationships in human life. It also prevents the premature narrowing of one's vision so that significant elements of situations are not overlooked. All of us have a very natural tendency to use our own experiences to define the significant elements of situations. The systems perspective helps us avoid this in several ways. It goes beyond individuals and looks, instead, at aggregates and networks of people. It illuminates the complex hierarchies of groups within which people live their lives, even though some of the larger groups' effects on individual behavior are only indirect. For example, the workings of Congress affect each of us even though we do not participate in it directly. The same is true of large, multinational corporations like General Motors and the major oil companies. The systems perspective also helps us to see that, as social workers, what we do is part of larger helping efforts — an agency, a profession, and the social welfare institution at a minimum. The linkages a systems perspective brings to our awareness makes it easier to understand why social workers study things like social policy and social research. Policy allows us to analyze and participate in larger economic and political systems so that we can use those systems in our helping efforts. Research enables us to obtain and use information so that we can make better-informed practice decisions. It also permits us to feed information to social planners, legislators, social agency directors, and other decision makers. Such information can help them understand the need for resources to help practitioners do their jobs better. Finally, a systems view broadens the scope of practice actions. Although help may be sought by one individual or a small group of individuals, we understand how their needs are part of larger systems. Successful intervention necessitates action at all of the levels involved in meeting needs. This, of course, is simply a different way of expressing social work's commitment to helping people function more effectively in their environment.

Human Diversity.   The human diversity perspective is another tool that can be used to broaden the social worker's view. People bring many kinds of differences to the situations they confront — differences that naturally influence their expectations, their behaviors, and their interactions. Therefore the same situation becomes a different experience for diverse people. Analyzing the situation accurately means being able to understand the way it is perceived and experienced by the particular people involved in it. The dominant values of a society often make it appear that there is only one reality in any situation and develop expectations around that view of reality. The human diversity perspective helps the social worker avoid such simplistic thinking, making it clear that there are many different realities for the various people involved in a situation. Imposing uniform expectations inevitably disadvantages some of these people — sometimes minimally, sometimes substantially.

In order to help people function more effectively in their environment, areas of conflict and strategies for their resolution must be understood. The human diversity perspective makes this possible by identifying the sources of differences, the ways differences are expressed, and points at which differences between people can be resolved or accommodated. Social policy becomes a very important arena for discussion of and decision making about the needs of different groups. The social worker has to seek fair representation from all groups in this process. Otherwise policies may be created that force the social worker to ignore the needs of certain groups or to respond to those needs in ways he or she knows will be unsuccessful. Research data are often a significant tool for analyzing the impact of various policies on diverse groups, as well as demonstrating the need for certain kinds of policies. An understanding of human diversity also helps the social worker avoid the tendency to impose his or her own values and views of reality on others. Social workers must understand *why* people act in different ways if they are ever to respect these differences, and they must treat human differences as potential sources of strength rather than as undesirable behavior to be eliminated.

Goal-Directed Behavior.   Human purpose gives direction to behavior. While human diversity helps us understand that different groups may formulate purposes differently, the goal-directed behavior perspective reminds us that human behavior is purposeful no matter what its particular form. The systems perspective is closely linked to the goal-directed perspective in that it provides a way of analyzing the contexts within which purposeful behavior occurs. Seeing behavior as goal-directed is important for social workers for several reasons. Random behavior is very difficult to understand and modify. The ability to see how behavior is patterned and organized around goals helps practitioners plan more effectively their own helping efforts. Just as importantly, seeing behavior as goal-directed helps the social worker understand what parts of the environment need to be included in efforts to improve the transactions between the people involved and their environment. Finally, understanding how people work toward goals helps practitioners respect their efforts. Social workers cannot always agree with the strategies people select to reach their goals. Similarly the goals themselves cannot always be supported given the profession's commitment to upholding certain societal and professional values and procedures. However, professional helping has to start with an understanding of what people are trying to accomplish, and this must be grounded in respect for their right to plan their own life goals.

Social work, then, is a profession in which knowledge and practice are inseparable: we have to *know* in order to *do*. The more we do the more knowledge we obtain so that future action will be more precise and better-informed. The profession's roots are deep in the liberal arts from which biological, behavioral, and social science concepts are derived. It is these concepts that comprise the knowledge base of social work, a base that is enriched as concepts are tested and refined in practice. Obviously the process of expanding knowledge from the liberal arts and from practice is an ongoing one. Yet if we adopt an ecological approach to professional practice, can we genuinely say our knowledge base is sufficient to support always effective intervention at both the individual and institutional levels? Have we a sufficient knowledge base to help form alternative institutions? to humanize existing ones? These questions will occupy the profession for some time to come. However, as in most systems, the profession's boundaries are permeable. It is constantly incorporating new perspectives, trying out new ideas, and responding in creative and imaginative ways to both its members and its consumers.

Index